DISCARD

AMERICAN POLITICS
AND GOVERNMENT

AMERICAN
POLITICS
AND
GOVERNMENT

ESSAYS IN ESSENTIALS

Edited by STEPHEN K. BAILEY

BASIC BOOKS, INC., PUBLISHERS
New York *London*

The Authors

CHARLES R. ADRIAN, Chairman, Department of Political Science, Michigan State University

ROBERT S. BABCOCK, Professor of Political Science, University of Vermont

STEPHEN K. BAILEY, Dean and Professor of Political Science, Maxwell Graduate School of Citizenship and Public Affairs, Syracuse University

JAMES MACGREGOR BURNS, Chairman, Department of Political Science, Williams College

DOUGLASS CATER, Special Assistant to the President, The White House

ROBERT A. DAHL, Professor of Political Science, Yale University

MERLE FAINSOD, Professor of Government, Harvard University

JOSEPH P. HARRIS, Professor of Political Science, University of California, Berkeley

DONALD HERZBERG, Executive Director, Eagleton Institute of Politics, and Professor of Political Science, Rutgers University

STANLEY KELLEY, JR., Professor of Politics, Princeton University

EARL LATHAM, Professor of Political Science, Amherst College

AVERY LEISERSON, Chairman, Department of Political Science, Vanderbilt University

ROY C. MACRIDIS, Professor of Political Science, University of Buffalo

GERARD J. MANGONE, Associate Dean, Maxwell Graduate School, and Professor of Political Science, Syracuse University

ROSCOE C. MARTIN, Professor of Political Science, Syracuse University

THE AUTHORS

ALPHEUS T. MASON, McCormick Professor of Jurisprudence, Princeton University

HANS J. MORGENTHAU, Professor of Political Science, University of Chicago

HUGH DOUGLAS PRICE, Associate Professor of Political Science, Syracuse University

CLINTON ROSSITER, Professor of American Institutions, Department of Government, Cornell University

E. E. SCHATTSCHNEIDER, Professor of Political Science Emeritus, Wesleyan University

HERMAN M. SOMERS, Professor of Politics and Public Affairs, Princeton University

Preface

An academic discipline is known by the questions it asks. It is known also by the methods it uses in finding answers. Even a cursory reading of the following essays suggests that the discipline of political science asks a variety of questions and uses a highly eclectic method in deriving answers. The general subject matter of political science, of course, centers on man's relationship to political authority. As Professor Dahl indicates in the first essay, for centuries men have been fascinated by the phenomenon of political authority. He then notes some of the recurring questions:

> How do we acquire knowledge about politics and about political life? How do we distinguish politics from other aspects of human life? In what ways are political systems similar to one another? In what ways do political systems differ from one another? What is the role of authority and power in political system? How do men behave in politics? What are the special characteristics, if any, of *homo politicus,* political man? What kinds of conditions make for stability, for change, or for revolution in a political system? What is required if social peace is to be maintained and violence to be avoided? What sort of political system is the best? How should we and how do we decide questions about what is "the best" in politics?

This, of course, is not a definitive list. But Professor Dahl's posing of these sample questions is perhaps sufficient to indicate the diversity and the range of political science curiosity. And the questions indicate how relevant political issues are to the lives and fortunes of all mankind—past, present, and future.

Over the centuries students of politics have differed in their answers to these and related questions. In recent times, and especially in the twentieth century as political science has emerged as a discrete academic discipline, differences about answers have been matched by differences about method. And differences about method have in turn shaped the questions that defenders of various methodological approaches have been prepared to tackle. For example, some political scientists maintain that many traditional questions about politics cannot be answered by using analytic tools which conform to modern canons of scientific inquiry. "What sort of political system is best?" is such a question. So is the question, "Should the American party system become more centralized?" These are, according to this particular school of political science, matters of preference—matters of value. A true political scientist, some claim, should not ask such questions because values cannot be "proved." Values can be examined as political data, but the values themselves are incapable of scientific verification. "In the 1960 presidential election, more Negroes voted for the Democratic presidential candidate than voted for the Republican candidate" is a statement of fact about the value preferences of Negroes which can be verified by an analysis of Negro voting districts. But the question "*Should* Negroes have voted for the Democratic presidential candidate" is not amenable to scientific inquiry. It therefore has no appropriate place in the discipline of political science.

Those who approach political science in this way find that many of their colleagues refuse to be so contained.

viii

Modern political science is such a rich amalgam of history, speculative philosophy, and behavioral science that it is effectively impossible for any one methodological school to pre-empt the field. Intuition, introspection, historical and literary analogy, metaphysical and theological speculation and deduction—these and other fashions of the mind are employed by many political scientists to "validate" their propositions. If these fashions of the mind have serious limitations as instruments for communicating acceptable proof, they at least have the advantage of keeping alive a number of questions that appear to many people to be of inestimable importance to the quality of human existence. While behavioral scientists improve their analytic tools—including a panoply of mathematical instruments and constructs—other social scientists and humanists will continue to make less rigorous and intuitive judgments as working propositions about what is true and what is good in political life.

Those, then, who look in the following essays for the methodological rigor of the behavioral scientists will in part be disappointed—although most of the essays reflect the substantial contributions to political knowledge that have been made by the more scientifically inclined in the profession. Some of the essays reflect strong value premises. No editorial attempt has been made to ensure that these value premises are consistent throughout the volume. Any such attempt would have been inconsistent with the original intent of the series: to reflect the rich diversity of opinion that exists about political matters within the discipline of political science as it is pursued and practiced in the United States. The hallmark of a free and pluralistic society is academic, as well as political, controversy.

If American political scientists can roughly be categorized according to the degree of their devotion to particular methods of analysis, they can also be categorized according to subdisciplines within the general field of political science. Most of the distinguished contributors to this particular series of essays are specialists in American government. But almost all large university departments of political science in the United States offer five or six "fields" within the discipline, of which American Government is only one. The most common titles used for the other political science fields are Political Theory, International Relations, Comparative Government, Constitutional Law, Political Parties, Political Behavior, State and Local Government, and Public Administration. The problem of classifying subfields in the discipline becomes obvious, however, when one recognizes that most of the subfields overlap. Functional specializations often cut across national boundaries. Even within national boundaries, politics, law, theory, and administration have no clear perimeters.

What can be said, however, is that each contributor to this series has written, thought, and taught intensively and extensively about the matters contained in his particular chapter. The topics were assigned by the editor with these special competencies in mind. The sum of the topics does not, of course, exhaust the several fields, interests, courses, and research specializations of the political science fraternity. There is, for example, no systematic treatment of the development of political theory or of public administration. Many countries and areas of the world are not mentioned. The choice of specific topics was necessarily arbitrary.

But with these inevitable caveats, the essays do have a central design. Together they do illuminate for the mature but relatively uninitiated reader the broad outlines of the American governmental and political system.

They attempt to place the American system in both a historical and a contemporary world perspective. The reader should come away with a sense of the questions that interest political scientists in the United States and the answers that have come to careful and sophisticated observers of American political institutions and political processes. None of the essays are works of pioneering research. The mandate to the contributors was to construct in readable fashion a series of essays that would summarize the best of their own and other scholars' research in the topics assigned.

The portrait of American political institutions that emerges from the separate chapters is, on the whole, a heartening one. The grand design of the founding fathers, as sketched by Professor Kelley, has had the structural strength of steel—the critical capacity to bend without breaking. No instrument of continuity and adaptability has been more fundamental to the success of the American experiment than the Supreme Court, as Professor Mason has pointed out. And yet the focal point of political leadership, according to Professors Rossiter and Somers, has been the person and the institution of the President.

If the essays on Congress by Professors Burns, Harris, and Price suggest some of the continuing problems of a separation-of-powers form of constitutional democracy, they also suggest the vital and positive roles played by the American national legislature in building consensus and in protecting minority as well as majority interests.

The four chapters by Professors Schattschneider, Herzberg, Latham, and Mr. Cater illuminate the kaleidoscopic and the often inchoate character of the political process. They also illustrate the role that public opinion, the press, and private interest groups play in the formulation of policy and in supplementing the more formal roles of parties and elections in the representative process.

The continuing vitality of state and local government in America is sometimes open to question and is a perennial subject for political debate. But Professors Martin, Babcock, and Adrian remind us that federalism is still a real and active force in American political life and is both a cause and effect of the freedoms we cherish.

An obvious fact of the twentieth century is that American political institutions and forces are inextricably related to those operating in other nations and in the collectivities of nations that have banded together in the United Nations and in regional alliances. But the nature of these linkages and relationships is often misunderstood. Professors Morgenthau, Mangone, Macridis, and Fainsod help us to understand our own political system by describing the ways in which other nations— singly and together—attempt to answer questions of order, freedom, and growth and how, in the process, the United States is inevitably affected. Finally, Professor Leiserson relates government and politics to the greatest cultural revolution in man's history: the explosive growth of science and technology which has marked the twentieth century.

If each of the authors should list his total indebtedness for the ideas and facts in his chapter, the preface would be longer than the rest of the book. But the editor can and must thank the authors themselves for the time, energy, and thought they have given to the production of these essays. They have generously agreed to contribute any royalties to the American Political Science Association in token of the services it has performed to the profession generally and to each of them individually. The skill of the authors in the preparation of the original manuscripts left the editor virtually unemployed, at least in his editorial capacity.

The editor especially thanks Mr. Theodore Wertime of the Voice of America, whose patience, understanding, guidance, and tact were exemplary.

Finally, to Mrs. Marian Borst a word of deep appreciation for expertness in manuscript preparation and for countless hours of bird-dogging.

The editor assumes responsibility for any and all mechanical errors. Responsibility for errors in fact, interpretation, and judgment must be borne by the individual authors. The editor, who knows all of the authors personally, cannot believe that this final responsibility will fall with any substantial weight upon shoulders which carry such remarkable heads.

Syracuse, New York   STEPHEN K. BAILEY
January 1965

Contents

CONTENTS

AMERICAN POLITICS
AND GOVERNMENT

1 WHAT IS POLITICAL SCIENCE?

Robert A. Dahl

What is political science?

To begin, political science is, of course, the study of politics. One might better say, it is the *systematic* study of politics, that is, an attempt by systematic analysis to discover in the confusing tangle of specific detail whatever principles may exist of wider and more general significance.

At the very outset, then, we must distinguish political science as the systematic *study* of politics from the *practice* of politics.

The same person may of course both study and practice politics. The student of politics may serve as an adviser to the political practitioner. Plato, the great Greek philosopher and political theorist, is said to have gone to Syracuse, in Sicily, in 367 B.C. to advise the ruler of that city—who, I am sorry to say, was a tyrant. Plato's equally renowned student, Aristotle, may have been a counselor to another ruler, Hermias; at any rate, Aristotle married the adopted daughter of Hermias, and it is difficult to imagine that the son-in-law, who took all knowledge as his province, neglected to pass on advice to his father-in-law. Philip of Macedon later engaged Aristotle to tutor his young son; Aristotle taught the son for six years during which time the boy became the young man. The young man's name was Alexander, known to us as Alexander the Great. What Alexander gained from his association with Aristotle is not known, nor is the converse.

Sometimes, though less often, a political scientist may be not only an adviser but also an active practitioner of the political arts. That astounding man of the Italian Renaissance, Niccolò Machiavelli, served as a secretary of the Republic of Florence for fourteen years. He was involved in diplomatic missions to popes, emperors, and kings; at the end of that time, like many politicians before and since, he was removed from office. That he was a victim of Florentine factionalism was a source of profound unhappiness to Machiavelli but is fortunate for us, for he whiled away the time that now hung so heavily on his hands by writing such masterpieces of political science as *The Prince* and *The Discourses* and even a great comic and rather scabrous play, *La Mandragola*. Machiavelli's descriptions and prescriptions are so lacking in ordinary standards of morality that his name has come to be associated with notions of ruthless egoism in politics. To many people, I imagine, he represents the essence of political evil. Yet the man himself loathed despotism and believed devoutly in the virtues of republican institutions. If his descriptions of politics seem to us immoral, it is partly because politics itself can be immoral; and in Renaissance Italy, as Machiavelli knew from his own direct observation, political practice was synonymous with ruthless egoism. Machiavelli regretted this fact perhaps as much as any man, but he sought to report honestly what he believed to be the truth. Alas, he has been condemned ever since for his truthfulness. He must have known from the fate of Socrates that the search for truth about politics does not always make one popular.

Machiavelli began his career as a politician and became a political scientist when his political career ended; with Woodrow Wilson the sequence was just the reverse. Wilson was a historian and political scientist long before he began the political career that propelled him into the White House. A book on Congress that he wrote as a young man is still widely read in the United States. Another and more mature book contained much sound wisdom about the relations of a President to the United States Senate on matters of foreign policy. It has sometimes been said that Wilson himself unfortunately ignored his own advice when he became President. But the practicing politician often does ignore the political scientist—even, as in Wilson's case, when the political scientist happens to be himself.

I mention these examples less to show that political scientists are typically involved in politics than the contrary. I want to emphasize that actually engaging in politics is not at all the same thing as studying politics in order to develop principles of general relevance. Political science means the study, not the practice, of politics.

As you may have noticed from these examples, the study of politics is an ancient field of learning. It is also a study that has received unusual emphasis in those Western cultures that derive from the worlds of Greek and Roman civilization. For the Greeks and Romans were immensely concerned with political things.

The modern study of politics, in fact, can be traced to that magnificent and unbelievably creative people, the Greeks of the fifth and the fourth centuries before Christ and, most of all, to the Athenians. It was in Athens that Socrates, Plato, and Aristotle raised to the highest level of intellectual endeavor the kinds of ques-

3

tions about politics that concern thoughtful men down to the present day. I have in mind such questions as:

How do we acquire knowledge about politics and about political life? How do we distinguish politics from other aspects of human life? In what ways are political systems similar to one another? In what ways do political systems differ from one another? What is the role of authority and power in political systems? How do men behave in politics? What are the special characteristics, if any, of *homo politicus*, political man? What kinds of conditions make for stability, for change, or for revolution in a political system? What is required if social peace is to be maintained and violence to be avoided? What sort of political system is the best? How should we and how do we decide questions about what is "the best" in politics?

Every age has produced one or two men who provide great answers to these great questions. I have mentioned the three Greeks: Socrates, Plato, and Aristotle. Let us consider several others. Cicero, who was both witness to and participant in the death agony of the Roman Republic; St. Augustine, born in North Africa in the fourth century; St. Thomas Aquinas, born near Naples in the thirteenth century; Machiavelli, born in Florence in the fifteenth century; Thomas Hobbes, the Englishman, born in the next century; John Locke, also an Englishman, born in the seventeenth century; at the end of the seventeenth century, a Frenchman, Montesquieu, who greatly influenced the men who drafted the United States Constitution; in the eighteenth century, another Frenchman, Rousseau; in the nineteenth century the Germans, Hegel, Marx, and Engels, the Englishmen Jeremy Bentham and John Stuart Mill, the Frenchman Alexis de Tocqueville. I had better stop; my list is

4

already long, yet I have omitted the names of several dozen men who, it could be argued with justice, have an equal claim to be numbered among the great political scientists of the ages. My point is simply that the kinds of questions that were first explicitly posed in the Western world by the Greeks have continued throughout the succeeding millennia to attract the gifted minds of every age.

Now I should like to examine our question, "What is political science?", a little more closely. Let me divide the question into the two suggested by the words "political" and "science." First, what is politics? Second, what is intended by the word "science," or "a scientific study of politics"?

What is politics? This innocent question is rather like asking a biologist, "What is life?" Biology, it is said, is the science of life or living matter in all its manifestations. Very well. But what is living matter? It turns out that this question is extremely difficult to answer and that biologists do not exactly agree on the answer. Yet they are quite confident that some kinds of matter—one-celled animals, for example—are clearly at the center of biology, while others—a piece of granite, for example— are clearly outside the field. So, too, in political science. We pretty well agree on the kinds of things that are definitely political. Thus the governments of the United States, the Soviet Union, and any other nation, province, state, city, town, or colony are unquestionably political and therefore in the domain of political science. The government of an ant colony is not; at any rate I have not noticed any of my colleagues writing about party politics or imperialism in ant colonies. Yet if we can say with confidence what lies at the center of politics, we are, like the biologist confronted with the question of life, not so sure of the exact boundaries.

Let me therefore describe what is at the center. To begin, wherever we find politics, most authorities agree, we necessarily encounter human beings living together in some kind of an association. Thus the opening words of Aristotle's great book *The Politics*: "Observation shows us first that every polis or state is a species of association." Wherever we find politics we encounter some special relationship among the human beings living together, a relationship variously called "rule," "authority," or "power." To refer once again to Aristotle, the very first page of *The Politics* contains references to different kinds of authority, what distinguishes the authority of the statesman from the authority of the head of the household or of the master over his slave, and the like. Wherever we find politics we discover conflict and ways in which human beings cope with conflict. Indeed, when human beings live together in associations and create rules, authorities, or governments to deal with these conflicts, the very attempts to rule also help to generate conflicts. Which comes first, power or conflict, need not detain us; we find both conflict and power wherever human beings live together. Politics arises, then, whenever there are people living together in associations, whenever they are involved in conflicts, and wherever they are subject to some kind of power, rulership, or authority.

These phenomena exist everywhere, therefore politics is everywhere. But not all associations have equal power. You can very easily test this—though I strongly urge you not to try—by having your family, which is one association, attempt to take over your neighbor's property, which, I am sure, happens to be protected by a more powerful association, the national state in which you reside. The state is the association that has the greatest power within some particular territory. Thus

6

the *government* of the state is obviously at the very center of politics, and therefore of political science. And the various organized institutions that make up the government of a state—the executive, the legislature, the judiciary, regional organizations, provinces, and local governments—all involve politics.

There are associations, organizations, and institutions that help to determine what the organs of government actually do: what rules the government adopts and enforces. In the modern world the most important are obviously political parties, such as the Republican and Democratic parties in the United States, Conservatives, Labourites, and Liberals in Britain, the Communist party in the Soviet Union, and so on. In many countries the political parties are so influential that one can consider them as a kind of informal government that rules the rulers. Thus political parties are pretty clearly at or near the center of politics and therefore of political science.

In addition to the parties, other organizations help to determine what the state does, even though they may not run candidates in elections and are not directly and openly represented in parliament. These associations are sometimes called interest groups; any association that tries to secure from the state policies favorable to its members or followers is an interest group. In the United States interest groups include such organizations as the American Medical Association, which represents physicians and has been involved in the struggle over a national program of medical care; labor unions, including the great national organization, the AFL–CIO, which frequently descends on Congress in an attempt to secure legislation favorable to trade unions in particular and the working people in general; farm organizations, which seek to gain favorable treatment for farms. One

7

could go on endlessly simply listing examples of interest-group organizations in the United States. Not long ago the United States House of Representatives debated and passed a bill increasing the legal authority of the federal government to protect the rights of Negroes. A recently published list[1] of the groups who were actively working in Washington to persuade congressmen to support the bill shows: six civil rights organizations, fifteen labor unions, nineteen religious organizations, and ten other groups.

Neither can we ignore ordinary citizens. Elections, voting, and other forms of participation by citizens in civic life are also elements of politics.

Have we now reached the boundaries of politics? Hardly. In fact, some political scientists would extend the meaning of politics to include *any* activity involving human beings associated together in relationships of power and authority where conflicts occur. In this sense, politics truly does exist everywhere: within trade unions, within the interest-group organizations of doctors or farmers, in business organizations, even in private clubs, indeed anywhere that human beings assemble together. Viewed in this way, the domain of politics and therefore of political science docs not stop simply with the institutions of the state, or even with such familiar political institutions as political parties and organized interest groups, but extends to an enormous range of human activity. The question of how far the boundaries of political science extend is a lively one among political scientists at the present time, but we need not linger over it any more. For it is perfectly obvious that no matter how they draw their boundaries, political scientists have more than enough to do.

1 *Congressional Quarterly*, 22 (February 21, 1964), 364.

What then of the second word? In what sense is the study of politics a science? In what sense *can* it be? Even if it can be, should it be a science? These questions, as you might imagine, are also the subject of a great deal of discussion; it is not too much to say that the discussion has gone on for a very long time, if not, in fact, from the time of the Greeks.

The term "science" has, course, many meanings. And the word does not mean quite the same thing in one language as it does in another. In some countries, scholars do not consider that political science is a single subject, like biology, but many subjects. Some scholars speak not of political science but of the political *sciences*. In France, until recently, one heard of *les sciences politiques* and in Italy *le scienze politiche*—that is, the political sciences. What do we mean, then, by *the science* of politics? To some people the word "science" simply means any systematic approach to human knowledge, so that one could speak of the science of physics, the science of mathematics, or perhaps even a science of theology. To others, and this is a good deal more common in English-speaking countries nowadays, the word "science" tends to be restricted to the natural sciences, studies that involve the observation of nature and the development of laws and theories explaining the phenomena of nature such as chemistry, physics, and the biological sciences. In recent years, particularly in the United States, we have come to speak of the social and behavioral sciences, that is, those that seek by observation to develop explanations of human behavior.

To confuse the matter even more, science is thought of sometimes as an achievement in being, sometimes as a method, and sometimes as a goal.

Physics is a science in the first sense. When one speaks of physics as a "real" science, he probably does not mean that physicists are simply hoping to develop theories that someday will explain the nature of physical reality; he means that they already have such theories, and they are of impressive power to explain the physical world.

But science also refers to the *methods* by which scholars investigate their subject. One might say that a century ago medicine was not very "scientific" because its methods were extremely crude; it was difficult to distinguish the charlatan from the honest inquirer after medical knowledge. Today, on the contrary, medical research in the most advanced laboratories uses highly sophisticated methods of inquiry very much like those used in physics, chemistry, and biology. Yet almost everyone would agree that in its laws, theories, and explanations medicine is not so far advanced as, say, physics.

One might also think of science as a goal, as something to be arrived at by rigorous methods of inquiry, even if present knowledge is somewhat sparse.

In which of these three senses is the study of politics a science? Despite the fact that the best minds of every age have tended to turn their attention to the study of politics, as I pointed out above, certainly the study of politics is not an already achieved science like physics. We simply do not have a body of theories about political systems that enables us to predict the outcome of complex events with anything like the reliability that a physicist, a chemist, or even a biologist generally can predict the outcome of complex events in his field. If you believe that there is such a theory in politics, I am bound to say that you are, in my opinion, deluding yourself. It is true that from time to time a writer, sometimes even a great writer, has claimed that he possesses a full-fledged predictive science of politics. So far, however, no comprehensive theory of politics that undertakes to predict the outcome of complex events has stood the test of experience. The most notable modern example of failure is, I think, Marx. If you examine his predictions carefully and test them against actual developments, he proves to be wrong in so many cases that only those who regard Marxism as a kind of religion to take on faith, and against all evidence, can remain persuaded that it is a truly predictive scientific theory. Nonetheless, political scientists do have an enormous amount of knowledge about politics, much of it extremely reliable knowledge.

A great deal of attention in modern political science is placed on the use of procedures or methods that are more likely to yield reliable results. Let me cite a well-known example. As late as thirty years ago, the *Literary Digest,* then a leading American magazine, attempted to predict the outcome of the presidential election of 1936 by asking millions of Americans how they proposed to vote in the coming election. The editors made the usual, widespread, and, as it happens, false assumption that the number of people asked would be so huge as to ensure that the sample would be a pretty accurate mirror of all voters. For convenience the editors questioned people who were listed in the telephone directories. This was a fatal mistake. The United States was in the middle of its greatest depression; among the unemployed and the poor, many families did not have a telephone. Led astray by its methods and overly confident because it had literally millions of replies to its question, the *Literary Digest* predicted that the Republican candidate, a conservative who drew his support mainly from the well-to-do sections of the population, would win by a substantial margin. Instead, Franklin Roosevelt was elected by a crushing majority that was swelled by the votes of the poor and the unemployed.

The simple mistake made by the *Literary Digest* now

seems obvious; but the important point is that since 1936 methods for making surveys have become vastly more reliable. Although laymen find it puzzling and even unbelievable, the fact is that with a properly drawn sample of only a few thousand people we can develop conclusions with far more reliability than the *Literary Digest* could by asking millions of people. In that very election in which the *Literary Digest* failed so abysmally, Dr. George Gallup, whose name has since become a household word in this country, used a small but properly selected sample to predict almost exactly how great the error was going to be in the forecast made by the *Literary Digest*. The editors evidently were not convinced. Incidentally, the magazine collapsed shortly after the election; it had utterly destroyed its own reputation as an unbiased journal.

We can say, then, that political science is the study of politics by methods and procedures designed to give us the greatest reliability in a highly complex world. As a body of knowledge, modern political science is definitely not a highly perfected science like physics or chemistry. Our knowledge of politics is continually and rapidly growing; however, this knowledge is of varying degrees of reliability, for some of it is highly speculative and about as reliable as anything one is ever likely to learn about human beings.

What objects or phenomena do we actually study in political science? I have already mentioned most of these when I discussed the boundaries of politics, but let me now enumerate the main phenomena, the "objects" of political science. First, we study individual citizens, voters, leaders. Strange as it may seem, study of the ways in which individuals actually behave in politics is one of the newest developments in the field. It is true, of course, that the behavior of individuals in politics has never been ignored. Machiavelli's *The Prince* describes how many Renaissance political leaders did act and prescribes how they had to act if they were to succeed in the ruthless and tempestuous political jungle that was Renaissance Italy. Even though few writers had as much to say about the seamy side of political life as did Machiavelli, insights about man's political behavior are scattered in works over the centuries.

Our understanding of man has made a quantum jump since Sigmund Freud and the advent of modern psychology, psychoanalysis, and psychiatry made us all acutely aware of man's capacity for irrational, nonrational, impulsive, neurotic, and psychotic action—in politics, unfortunately, as much as elsewhere. Partly as a result of this change, in the last several decades political scientists have begun to observe individuals and politics with a concern for detail and accuracy that, if not entirely new, is at least highly uncommon. What is new, perhaps, is a search for reliable generalizations. We are no longer content to observe a few individuals engaged in politics and to describe their behaviors, to investigate a few great, unusual leaders or a few simple yet possibly rare citizens. Rather, we want to know how widely our generalizations apply.

In American politics, as you know, there are only two major parties, the Republicans and the Democrats. Many citizens are so loyal to one of these two parties that it is most unlikely that they would ever change their vote during a political campaign. Some citizens, however, have no strong loyalties to either of these two parties nor, in fact, to any party at all. It is a common belief that these people who do not feel strong loyalties either to the Democratic or Republican parties, the independent voters, tend to be the most thoughtful and reflective, the most attentive to what happens in campaigns, the most interested in the results. In short, the independent voter is often thought to be, at least by comparison, a model citizen, rational, thoughtful, responsible, open-minded, in contrast to the partisan who, it is often thought, is less reflective, less thoughtful, and perhaps even less interested in a campaign because he made up his mind long ago and nothing will budge him. The view is, surely, plausible. Beginning with the presidential election of 1940, however, studies by American social scientists began to destroy this happy picture of the independent voter. In one study after another it was discovered that, far from being a thoughtful, attentive, responsible citizen, a person who lacks any spirit of partisanship more than likely has no great interest in politics, is quite ignorant about politics, does not pay much attention to political campaigns, and makes up his mind at the last possible moment, frequently on the basis of rather trivial or accidental influences. This independent voter is likely to represent the classic case of the man who votes for Smith rather than Jones for no better reason than that he happens to overhear his barber or bartender speak confidently about Smith's virtues.

This finding has forced us to do some rethinking of our notions about the roles of partisan and independent in American politics and perhaps in democratic systems in general. We cannot yet be sure how widespread this phenomenon is. Some studies indicate that it holds in certain European countries, in nations as different, for example, as Britain and Italy. But it may not hold in others. A recent analysis suggests that perhaps our model citizen, the thoughtful, reflective, interested man who does not make up his mind until he has tried to hear both sides of the argument, does actually exist in the United States and may play no negligible role in elections, even though his numbers are pretty tiny.

A second phenomenon studied by political scientists is the private or semipublic associations to which many individuals belong. The most visible of these, as I suggested earlier, are political parties. There are a vast number of studies of political parties throughout the world: how they are organized, how nominations are made, what the parties do in campaigns and elections, the characteristics of party leaders, members, and followers, and differences and similarities in the party systems of various countries.

Perhaps the most significant development during the last several decades has been the discovery of the tremendous importance of interest groups, particularly in the United States. Because class lines are rather weak, vague, and uncertain in this country, despite considerable differences in social standing, prestige, and income, and because our political parties, unlike many European parties, are neither tightly organized nor highly centralized, it was natural, I suppose, that American political scientists were the first to turn their attention to interest groups. It is fair to say, in fact, that they pioneered investigation in this area. In the last decade, however, concern with the role of interest groups in politics has spread to European political scientists, who have also begun to demonstrate that social classes and political parties are by no means the only significant political forces in European politics and that a variety of interest groups are active in the political parties and influence cabinet ministers, the civil servants, and other governmental officials. It would be impossible to understand the operation of any democratic system if one ignored the decisive role often played by representatives of the variety of interests that exists in a modern industrialized and urbanized society.

A third focus for study is of course the political institutions themselves—the parliaments, the cabinets, the courts, the civil service, and the like. These are such obvious and familiar subjects for political science, therefore, that I will not comment on them further.

A fourth focus is a political system as a whole. A lively question of enduring interest to American political scientists is how to distinguish democracies from other systems and, perhaps more important, what conditions are required for the stability of democratic institutions. As political scientists learn more about the actual operation of democratic political systems, it becomes obvious that the gap between the ideals formulated by classical spokesmen for democracy, such as Locke, Rousseau, and Jefferson, are not only a long way from achievement (a fact that in itself would hardly be a new discovery) but may even have to be reformulated for fear that, as unattainable and utopian goals, they serve merely to discredit democracy as an ideal.

The existence of many new nations only recently liberated from colonial rule and still struggling with problems of independence, internal peace, and self-government presents as great an intellectual challenge to political scientists as they have ever faced: to discover the conditions under which these countries can develop stable constitutional governments based on the consent and support of the bulk of the population and capable of an orderly solution to staggering problems of economic growth and social development. It is fair to state that the study of politics in its 2,000-year development in the West has been rather parochial.

Now that we are confronted by the need for moderately reliable knowledge about the political systems developing in Africa, Asia, and even in Latin America, we find that facts and theories drawn from the experience of European and English-speaking countries are inadequate. As a consequence, during the last decade or so tremendous efforts have been made in the United States to develop scholars with an understanding of the problems and politics of the non-Western world. It is ironical that with characteristic American enthusiasm for new causes this effort has moved so rapidly that today one hears increasing talk of our failure to improve our knowledge of Europe. We are producing, it is sometimes said, more specialists on Burma or Ghana than on France and Italy, for example. In a world where events in any nation, no matter how small or remote, can significantly affect what happens tomorrow to all of us, demands on human knowledge are overwhelming and the need for knowledge outstrips our frail human capacities.

I must discuss one other focus of political science that is so painfully important to all of us that it might even be placed at the very center of the stage. I have in mind, of course, the relationships among political systems, that is, international relations. Here, too, the challenge strains our capacities to the very limit if not, indeed, beyond. In their attempt to grapple with the portentous and enormously complicated problems of international politics, political scientists in recent years have resorted to an amazing variety of techniques of inquiry and analysis, not excluding even the use of electronic computers to simulate negotiation and conflict among several countries in international politics. Although some of these efforts might seem absurd and unrealistic, my view is that we are so desperately in need of solutions that we can ill afford to mock any serious intellectual effort to discover them; and help may come from quite unexpected quarters.

These, then, are some of the phenomena studied by modern political scientists. You might want to know *how* we study these things? To answer this question properly would require many chapters. Politics, as everyone knows, is not something one can directly observe in either a laboratory or a library. Indeed, direct observation of politics is often extremely difficult or downright impossible. Consequently, we often have to study politics by indirect observation, through historical materials, records, papers, statistical data, and the like. This process, I have no doubt, conveys the customary image of near-sighted scholars consulting the works of one another without ever emerging from the library into the heat and turmoil of political life. Yet one of the oldest though often neglected traditions of political science is the tradition of direct observation.

It is worth recalling that the great Greek students of politics, Socrates, Aristotle, and Plato, were able to and did observe politics in the compact laboratory of the city-state. They did not make the sharp division that modern scholars often make between the world of books and study and the world of affairs. Eighteen centuries later, Machiavelli was able to observe the political life of Renaissance Italy from his post in the Republic of Florence. I rather think there are many scholars today who believe that their fragile dignity would be damaged should they leave their libraries to mingle with the ordinary folk in the noisy byways of politics. Nonetheless, a most interesting development over the last several decades has been the growing insistence that wherever possible the scholar should observe as directly as he can the objects of his study. As a result, never before in history have there been so many scholars seeking to interview politicians, civil servants, and ordinary citizens.

It is only a slight exaggeration to say that if you were to visit the United States Congress today the chances are that the man you pass in the corridor will be not a congressman but a political scientist. This development is, in my view, an enormously healthy one, for just as the biologist is no less a biologist, but a good deal more, because he observes in his laboratory the organisms with which he works, and just as the physician gains knowledge from studying patients and not merely from reading what others have written about disease, so too the study of political science has gained from the growing conviction that one cannot know politics merely by traversing the path between the classroom and the library. Yet to observe politics directly is much more difficult for us than it was for Aristotle or for Machiavelli; for the world we study is larger and more complicated, the population is greater, and the slice of the world we see —we now know—is not likely to be truly representative of the world.

The political scientist's laboratory, then, is the world —the world of politics. And he must work in that laboratory with the same caution and the same rigorous concern for the accuracy and reliability of his observation that is true of the natural scientist in his laboratory; with a good deal less chance, nonetheless, of succeeding. Because direct observation is no simple matter of casual and accidental interview, the political scientist finds that for every hour he spends observing politics he may have to spend a dozen analyzing his observations. Raw observations are all but useless, so the scholar still must work at his desk, in the silence of his study, reading and reflecting, trying to pierce the veil that seems always to keep truth half-hidden. Now that we have brought our political scientist back to his desk, far from the hurly-burly of politics, let us leave him there. But if he is to study politics he cannot stay there long. You may run into him at the next political meeting you attend.

2 THE AMERICAN CONSTITUTIONAL SYSTEM

Stanley Kelley, Jr.

In this chapter I shall discuss some basic features of the American constitutional system and some of its founders' purposes.

I shall devote time to the second item because I am convinced that it helps one to understand the first. I believe, and I think I can show, that a knowledge of the outlook and objectives of the men who wrote the federal Constitution is a good introduction to understanding American governmental institutions and practices as they exist now, even though modern American government is vastly more complex and more extensive in its exercise of powers than anything envisioned in 1787. A knowledge of its origins contributes a great deal to understanding the government of the United States, because, like the governments of many of today's new nations but unlike those of many older states, it was a deliberate creation at a point in time. Its principal institutions were set up all at once, by particular men, with particular purposes in mind. It was a government that came into being by design. To appreciate a painting, it is helpful to know what the painter had in mind; so to understand the American constitutional system, it is useful to know something of the purposes of those who planned it.

It is useful, of course, only if what the founders built resembles what they hoped to build. There can be little doubt, however, that American government is in many important respects what its architects intended it to be. The writing of constitutions inherently involves making predictions about what institutions that do not yet exist will be like when they do. The predictions of this kind that America's founding fathers made and the reasoning on which they based them are at least partly a matter of record. It is a record that makes it quite evident that the most articulate of the founders—Hamilton and Madison, particularly—not only knew what they wanted but also had remarkably realistic notions about how they could get what they wanted. Although some of their predictions were wrong, in general their notions about the way the new government would work in practice have been borne out by experience.

I should make one more thing clear about the manner in which I am approaching this subject. I have been speaking of *the* purposes of the founders, what *they* wanted. Of course, they differed among themselves in both interests and objectives. Frequently, in fact, discussions of the writing of the Constitution are devoted mainly to the conflicts that attended it. Serious differences did arise in the Constitutional Convention—between the representatives of northern and southern states, between those who spoke for small states and large ones, between slaveowners and nonslaveowners, between those who wanted a weak and those who wanted a strong Executive power. These differences were resolved, however, in the interest of achieving ends that the founders considered of overriding importance, in the interest of objectives they shared. It is these shared objectives that I want to stress here, just as the founders did in their actions.

What were the founders seeking to do? First of all, they wanted a strong central government for the thirteen American states. At least they wanted a stronger government than that which existed at the time they met to consider revision of the Articles of Confederation. They wanted a government that could act positively and forcefully. They wanted it because they had seen, or thought they had seen, the consequences of weak government.

Between the close of the American Revolution and the adoption of the new Constitution, the states of the Union suffered losses in foreign trade. British and West Indian ports were closed to American shipping. Interstate trade was hampered by state tariff barriers and by differing state currencies. In the West, settlers were inadequately protected from the Indian tribes. Men who looked to the general government to remedy these evils saw a "government" that negotiated treaties in the name of a Union of states, only to have them ignored by states individually; a government with an empty treasury; a government regarded as so unimportant by many of the members of its own legislative body that they did not bother to attend legislative sessions. By General Washington, hero of the Revolution, it was characterized as "a half-starved limping government that appears almost to be moving upon crutches and tottering at every step." It was in fact more the Secretariat and Council of a league of independent states than a true governing body. It had not and probably could not have done what Washington and other founders wanted it to do: take *action*, action that would effectively preserve internal order, promote trade, and win the respect of foreign nations.

If forceful government was one major objective of the writers of the American Constitution, limited government was another.

The notion of limited government, at least in American thought, has taken on a corona that does as much to obscure as to illuminate its meaning. I think it meant something reasonably simple to most practical men in 1787. It meant that government ought not to do some things. It ought not, for one thing, to abridge certain personal rights and legal protections of such rights. The Constitution as originally written, reflecting this sentiment, prohibits legislating penalties for individuals and punishing men for acts that are crimes only retroactively; it also limits to exceptional circumstances the right of public officials to take citizens into custody without bringing them speedily to trial. The first ten amendments to the original Constitution, really a part of the Constitutional Settlement of 1788, are largely guarantees of personal liberties—of the rights to speak, assemble, publish, and worship freely; of the right of a fair trial; and of protection against arbitrary action by military authorities.

To the founders, limited government also meant protecting the rights of property; they have in fact sometimes been accused of having been more concerned with property rights than with the rights of persons. We cannot deny, however, that the founders considered the protection of property rights a fundamental purpose of all government. They said so again and again. They felt compelled to declare themselves on the subject so often, undoubtedly, because they distrusted—even feared—some of the political currents running at the time. At least some of the founders had little faith in the ability of existing state governments to protect property, and such faith as they did have had been shaken not long before by a rebellion in Massachusetts. It will be recalled that when the Massachusetts courts tried to enforce the collection of certain debts, Daniel Shays led debtors in revolt. The state militia, financed by private subscriptions of Boston merchants, were needed to quell the rebellion. Anyone reading *The Federalist*—which makes the case par excellence for the adoption of the Constitution—can hardly fail to be impressed by the great number of references to Shays's Rebellion and to the number of warnings that strong government was needed to prevent similar incidents in the future.

The apprehensions of the founders were at least partly the reason that they wrote into the Constitution the clauses forbidding states to issue paper money or to pass laws impairing the obligation of contracts. These provisions do not count for many words in the Constitution, but, in the opinion of James Madison, "the articles relating to treaties, to paper money, and to contracts, created more enemies than all the errors in the system, positive and negative, put together." These provisions of the proposed constitution created enemies, because they were directly related to live political conflicts.

A third purpose to which the writers of the Constitution were committed was the construction of a government that would be broadly representative, one that would be responsive to the great mass of citizens. Madison voiced the sentiments of many of the founders when he held it to be a principle of all good government that those bound by laws should help to make them. Other founders may have accepted the democratic principle less out of conviction than because they thought it practical politics to do so; in any event, they accepted it. Not to have done so would have doomed their enterprise from the beginning. Even though there were property qualifications for voting in most of the states at the time the Constitution was adopted, there seem to have been few adult males who were disenfranchised. The founders knew this. Whether or not the provisions of the Constitution would be acceptable to the mass of the voters who would vote on its ratification, therefore, was constantly in their minds.

One can say, then, that the founders of the American constitutional system wanted—or thought that they had to accept—a strong central government, a government that would not violate personal and property rights, and a broadly representative government.

They also knew that in practice these purposes could easily conflict. To make this fact as evident to us as it was to them, it is enough to ask two questions. How can one make a government strong enough to resist rebellion and to repel foreign invasions and yet ensure that it will not use that power to abridge either personal liberties or the rights of property? How can one give power to the great mass of the people who have little property and yet keep them from advancing their interests at the expense of the few who own a great deal of property?

The founders saw these questions as posing a problem, not a dilemma. The authors of *The Federalist* phrased it this way: "If men were angels, no government would be necessary. If angels were to govern men, neither internal nor external controls on government would be necessary. In framing a government which is to be administered by men over men, the great difficulty lies in this: You must first enable the government to control the governed, and in the next place oblige it to control itself."

How did the founders try to meet this difficulty? The grants of powers and guarantees of personal property rights that they wrote into the constitutional document itself did not meet it, and they did not see them as doing so. The founders entertained no illusions that the Constitution would be self-enforcing or that its provisions could be more than "parchment barriers"—the phrase is that of the authors of *The Federalist*—to tyrannical government. Rather, they tried to contrive a set of governmental institutions that would work as they wanted them to work, even if the men who held positions of official power did not wholly share their objectives. They tried to design a governmental machine that, even though manned by ambitious and self-regarding men, would function to promote general interests in the economic development and national security and protect the rights of persons and property.

To secure a stronger central government, the founders devised a federal system—a system that divided legal authority between the states and the Union. The very conception of federation stands as testimony to their capacity to innovate, for the federal system of government they devised had no close parallels in previous political history. The idea of federation is also testimony to their capacity to adjust what they proposed to do to what they thought could win acceptance. Modern Americans tend to regard federation as the best of all possible governmental schemes; it was not so regarded by the founders. They saw it as an expedient, a practical means to achieve the strongest central government possible.

Men more dogmatic and less politically sophisticated than the founders might well have concluded that it was an expedient that could not work. The founders themselves expected leaders at each of the two levels of government to attempt to encroach upon powers reserved to the other. They did not expect the division of authority between the states and the Union that they described in the Constitution—described quite vaguely in fact—to be any substantial impediment to such encroachment. How could they hope, then, that a division of powers could be maintained that would enable the central government to do what they wanted it to do? I think they counted principally on two things: that conflicts of interest *between* the state governments and the balance of power among them would often work in favor of the central government, and that the central government could attract enough popular support to make attempts to usurp its powers by state governments politically inexpedient for state officials. Making the general government the representative of mass opinion would help to make it strong, and the federal system, properly set up, its parts properly balanced against each other, would be self-maintaining.

The founders worked out the solution to their second principal problem—how to achieve strong and limited government simultaneously—in much the same spirit. They gave the central government ample power, but they divided it, giving parts of it to different and independently based departments. No one man or one branch was to be able to exercise all the powers of government.

They drew this formula partly from their own fund of political experience and partly from the French philosopher Montesquieu. They shared Montesquieu's belief that to put all the powers of government—legislative, executive, and judicial—into the same hands was to invite tyranny, and they believed with him that "it is necessary from the very nature of things that power be a check to power." This reflected on their part a certain pessimism—or realism, depending on one's point of view—about the men it is reasonable to expect in political life. They thought it imprudent to construct a government on the supposition that its officials would always be either good or wise.

The founders went a step beyond merely dividing powers of government. They made agreement among independent departments of government necessary if the government as such was to act. As Professor Neustadt indicated in *Presidential Power,* they created "a government of separated institutions *sharing* powers." Thus the President signs or vetoes the laws of Congress and nominates judges for appointment to the courts; the Congress empowers, or declines to empower, the executive departments to act; the Senate must confirm the President's nominations for appointment; and the courts may test the constitutionality of presidential acts or the acts of Congress.

John Adams, the second President of the United States, described with as great care as anyone these complex relationships of shared and balanced powers. As he put it: (1) the states are balanced against national government; (2) the House of Representatives is balanced against the Senate; (3) the Executive is balanced against the Legislature; (4) the Judiciary is balanced against the Executive and the Legislature; (5) the Judiciary is balanced against the states; (6) the Senate is balanced against the President; and (7) the people are balanced against the government.

Certainly this is one of the most intricate systems of government the founders could have seriously proposed. But the intricacies were for a purpose, as I have already suggested. They were intended to reconcile what can be reconciled in government only with great difficulty: strength, responsiveness to popular opinion, and protection for the rights of individuals. They were intended to reconcile these things and did, though whether they did so on the best terms will always be open to debate.

The government they created was a vigorous one— strong enough to insure public credit, to preserve internal order, to stabilize banking and currency, to defend the country against foreign enemies, and to open up the new land to the West for settlement.

It was a remarkably stable government. In 1789 there

was a king in France, a tsar in Russia, a Holy Roman emperor, a sultan in Turkey. The American Republic has outlived all. The office held today by President Lyndon Johnson is far more like that held by George Washington than the office held by Elizabeth II is like that of George III. Stability is not the only virtue of a government, but it is a virtue nonetheless. Stability can be purchased at too high a price but internal strife is costly too, costly in terms of economic development, costly in many other ways important to a nation's people.

The American governmental system, finally, has allowed popular opinion to shape its ends and individual rights to find protection within it, though this has not been achieved without strain and frustration and continuing debate.

The founders' scheme of government deprived the United States of any one branch or organ of government that could claim convincingly that it alone was the popular branch: The states, the President, and the Congress could all claim to reflect the popular will. The founders' scheme also made it likely that the various institutions of government would reflect the popular will differently. Officials in the different branches have different constituencies and those who are elected are chosen at different times and for different terms. They are all responsive to popular opinion, but not quite the same popular opinion and not quite in the same way.

In consequence, it is difficult for a majority that is not large and enduring to gain control of government and to legislate a program against opposition. Conversely, it is relatively easy for some minorities to check the will of the majority and to protect their interests. These minorities may be unpopular religious or political sects, sectional interests, or wealthy property owners.

What happened to the New Deal, certainly the most

thoroughgoing revolution in American politics in modern times, illustrates both the ultimate power of popular opinion in the United States and the short-run constraints that the American constitutional system places on it. The stock market, President Herbert Hoover's popularity, and public confidence in the Republican party fell off sharply in 1929. In 1930 the Democratic party won the right to organize the House of Representatives. The Democrats had to wait until 1933, however, before they controlled the Presidency and the Senate as well. When Franklin D. Roosevelt took office in that year, a Democratic Congress followed his lead in passing a sweeping legislative program. It did so, only to see a number of its key measures cut down by the Supreme Court. Not until after 1937 can one really count the New Deal as having been achieved. By that time it was a different New Deal—in the view of many, a New Deal older, wiser, and more moderate than it had been in 1932. I feel sure that that is the way many of the writers of the Constitution would have wanted it to have happened.

In none of what I have discussed have I meant to suggest that a knowledge of the origins of the American governmental system is sufficient to understand it, nor to deny that there have been important developments in that system that its founders neither intended nor foresaw. I have argued rather that knowing what the founders tried to do is a useful key to understanding the government of the United States and that the founders' grasp of what they were doing was substantial. The founders were in fact quite aware that their science of government was inexact and their design of government only a sketch. Hamilton, writing in *The Federalist,* said, "time only . . . can mature and perfect so compound a system, can liquidate the meaning of all the parts and can adjust them to each other in a harmonious and consistent whole."

I indicated at the outset that a discussion of the objectives and outlook of the men who wrote the Constitution of the United States was a good introduction to American government and politics. I should add now that this is true only if one also appreciates the fact that America's constitutional system is still being built.

3 THE ROLE OF THE SUPREME COURT

Alpheus T. Mason

The Supreme Court, as always, is in the news. On February 17, 1964, the justices asserted their responsibility for maintaining the democratic character of the American political process. Reaffirmed was America's bold commitment of 1776—that just governments rest not on coercion and force but on reason and consent. "As nearly as practicable," Justice Black wrote for the majority, "one man's vote in a Congressional election is to be worth as much as another"—in short, "one man, one vote."

The decision was not unanimous; three justices dissented, Justice Harlan roundly attacking his six colleagues for violating another basic American principle —separation of powers. Harlan charged that the Court had usurped power belonging exclusively to Congress.

As so often in the past, the differences in the already famous Georgia Reapportionment case turned less on substance than on the Court's role. All nine justices agreed that the Constitution requires each man's vote in congressional elections be measured by *some* fair standard; they disagreed on whether the Court could impose that standard without violating a fundamental principle of the Constitution. The cleavage in this most recent case illustrates a continuing controversy, dividing both

Court and country, on the scope of judicial power in the American system of free government.

The intricate design of our constitutionalism reflects James Madison's classic formulation: "In framing a government which is to be administered by men over men, the great difficulty lies in this: you must first enable the government to control the governed; and in the next place oblige it to control itself." For correctives against abuse of power, Americans have not been content to rely on political checks. Public opinion and the ballot box, the essential safeguards in most free societies, are not enough for us. "A dependence on the people," Madison remarked, "is no doubt, the primary control on government; but experience has taught mankind the necessity of auxiliary precautions." In America, government is kept within bounds not only by the electoral process but also through separation of powers, federalism, the vague "due-process-of-law" requirement, and, as an adjunct to all these, the well-nigh unique doctrine of judicial review.

Judicial review, but one of several devices limiting the power to govern, has not always been utilized in the service of democracy. Originally construed narrowly, judicial review was so exercised for nearly the first half-century of the nation's life. Between 1789 and 1836 the Supreme Court interpreted its power modestly. At the national level, we relied primarily on political restraints to secure us from tyrannical government.

As the composition of the Court varies, so does the nature and scope of judicial power. Chief Justice Marshall staunchly upheld national supremacy over conflicting state action. He was content to defer to "the wisdom and discretion of Congress," checked by the control voters possess at elections, as "the sole restraint" on congressional authority. Under the leadership of his successor,

Chief Justice Taney, the Court qualified Marshall's nationalistic jurisprudence. The effect was to elevate the judiciary, rendering it, ultimately, the arbiter of highly volatile issues, including slavery and federalism. In a reckless display of judicial pre-eminence, the Taney Court vetoed a major legislative policy, forestalling congressional effort to deal with slavery, thereby helping to precipitate the Civil War.

Hardly had the wounds of that tragic conflict started to heal when a postwar Court began to undo the spoils of victory. In a series of historic decisions based on the concept of nation-state equality—a notion thought to be forever repudiated by Union victory—the Supreme Court emasculated far-reaching legislation designed to secure the social and political rights of the newly emancipated Negro. So effectively did the justices undermine the bases of national authority in this area that almost a century elapsed before Congress again enacted civil rights legislation.

The post-Civil War decisions were but a prelude to an era of judicial supremacy. For nearly half a century (1890–1936), the Court successfully pitted its own prejudices against legislative attempts to regulate the excesses of a burgeoning industrialism. In 1895 the Court vetoed congressional effort to enact a federal income tax, embarrassed national attempts to enforce antitrust legislation, and frustrated organized labor's drive to make itself felt in our expanding economic life. In all these cases the Court intervened to protect the rights of private property against the humanitarian impulse of social reformers.

By 1936 the Supreme Court had seriously hampered the power to govern at both state and national levels. In a single term, 1935–1936, thirteen acts of Congress were set aside as invalid. At the term's end, one dissenting justice observed dourly: "We seem to have tied Uncle Sam up in a hard knot."

The high-level political war that ensued between President Franklin D. Roosevelt and the Court obscures the fact that the justices, without exception, regarded New Deal legislation with a jaundiced eye. On this point they were unanimous. Their differences concerned the Court's role in a free society.

Speaking for the majority, outlawing congressional control of agricultural production, Justice Roberts contended that upholding this Act would mean "legislative powers without restriction or limitation." Congress might become "a parliament of the whole people, subject to no restrictions save such as are self-imposed." Justice Stone, joined by two other dissenters, countered by asking the majority to consider the status of its *own* power. The Executive and Congress were limited, Stone pointed out, by "the ballot box and the process of democratic government," and "subject to judicial restraint; the only check on our own power is our own sense of self-restraint." The three dissenters went on to suggest that judicial aggrandizement had been carried to such lengths the Court had come to think of itself as "the only agency of government that must be assumed to have the power to govern."

This fierce battle among the justices highlights the distinction between judicial *review* and judicial *supremacy*. Under the guise of interpreting fundamental law, the Court had, in fact, made itself a superlegislature; it had denied Congress a power conferred by the Constitution. The basic inconsistency between popular government and judicial *supremacy* was underscored.

Justice Roberts' opinion demonstrates the limits to which this oligarchic element in our politics can be carried: judicial review inevitably runs the risk of becoming judicial supremacy. Justice Stone's urgent plea for self-restraint shows how this danger can be reduced to a minimum. When it became clear that dissenting opinions unwittingly bolstered the President's anti-Court charges, he exploited them for all they were worth. Finally, in the face of Roosevelt's threat to pack it, the Court retreated. Indeed, even as the Court-packing storm raged, and before any new appointments were made, the justices, discrediting their own precedents, upheld state and federal legislation recently suspect on constitutional grounds. The impasse between Congress and Court was thus resolved by the justices themselves.

Like the opposition party that finally wins an election, the Supreme Court after 1937 was faced with the necessity of probing for the limits of the undefined philosophy of judicial self-restraint. As to commercial regulations, this self-denying ordinance had been put into practice. Would the same narrow concept of judicial power apply to enactments curtailing freedom of speech, thought, and religion? An answer was soon forthcoming. In an otherwise obscure opinion of 1938, Justice Stone appended the now-famous footnote, suggesting that for legislation regulating the economy, judicial hands-off would henceforth be the rule, but in the orbit of civil rights the Court's responsibility was less confined. There would be narrower scope for the traditional presumption of constitutionality when legislation touched specific prohibitions mentioned in the Bill of Rights. Moreover, any legislation restricting those political processes that could ordinarily be expected to bring about repeal of undesirable legislation, any statutes directed against particular religious or national or racial minorities, would require *"more exacting judicial scrutiny."*

By 1943 the Court seemed to have endorsed these propositions, prompting Justice Jackson to observe: "If there is any fixed star in our constitutional constellation it is that no official, high or petty, can prescribe what shall be orthodox in politics, nationalism, religion, or other matters. . . . The very purpose of a Bill of Rights was to withdraw certain subjects from the vicissitudes of political controversy, to place them beyond the reach of majorities and officials and to establish them as legal principles to be applied by the courts." "We cannot," Jackson continued, "because of modest estimates of our competence in such specialties as public education, withhold the judgment that history authenticates as the function of this Court when liberty is infringed."

Like Thomas Jefferson, Jackson believed that freedom increased our national strength, that "government limited with respect to basic rights need not be anemic." The Justice went on to suggest that "without promise of a limiting Bill of Rights it is doubtful if our Constitution could have mustered enough strength to enable ratification. To enforce those rights today is not to choose weak government over strong government. It is only to adhere as a means of strength to individual freedom of mind in preference to officially disciplined uniformity for which history indicates a disappointing and disastrous end."

Jackson's position accords with the best in our heritage, but disagreement and opposition also fit our tradition. Former Justice Frankfurter believed that liberty is best maintained when instilled in the habits of the people and left to the "forum of public opinion." For Frankfurter judicial review limits popular government, overlooking the fact that the framers planned it that way. They insisted that the dependence of government on the people must not be carried to such extent that individual rights are left unprotected. Judicial review was "American democracy's way of covering its bet."

Substitution of judicial *supremacy* for judicial *review,* as in the years prior to 1937, created, as we have seen, a deadlock between Court and Congress. For a corrective the justices returned to the wisdom of the framers, to judicial humility. Once political controls had been re-established as the primary check on government, it seemed logically to follow that the Court must shoulder a corresponding responsibility for the effective function-ing of the political process itself. The Court's assumption of such responsibility has evoked a variety of responses. For certain justices, First Amendment freedoms are "preferred." More sacred than those of property and contract, these freedoms are protected from legislative encroachment not only by the due process requirement but also by the injunction that "Congress shall make *no* law . . . abridging the freedom of speech, or of the press; or the right of the people peaceably to assemble. . . ." The underlying thought seems to be that though the Constitution does not embody, as Justice Holmes said, any particular *economic* philosophy, it does incorporate a particular political theory. Central to that theory are the freedoms listed in the First Amendment. As to these, judicial self-restraint does not mean the Court is para-lyzed. "It simply conserves its strength to strike more telling blows in the cause of a working democracy."

Except for occasional deviations, the Court since 1937, and especially since the middle 1950s, has subjected to close scrutiny government action threatening civil rights. Evidence mounts that the "self-restraint" banner raised in 1937 has not blinded Chief Justice Warren to certain positive responsibilities. His Court began to discharge these responsibilities on May 17, 1954, that historic day when the justices handed down their unanimous judg-ment in the school segregation cases. The anxiously awaited opinion was short and incisive. "In approaching this problem," the Chief Justice remarked, "we must consider public education in the light of its full development and its present place in American life throughout the Nation." Segregation, he said, may affect hearts and minds in a way unlikely ever to be undone. Redressing the damage done civil rights legislation a century earlier, the Warren Court filled the gap other branches of government were unable or unwilling to close.

Racial segregation is not the only field in which the Warren Court has responded to a positive responsibility. At a single sitting, June 17, 1957, the justices shouldered other tasks in the civil rights orbit. Upheld was the right of anyone to advocate overthrow of the government, so long as the preaching does not openly urge specific action; qualified was the power of congressional committees to make investigations and require witnesses to testify; limited was the state's power to force witnesses to cooperate in investigations authorized by state law. In 1961 the justices, reversing a position of only a decade earlier, ruled that unlawfully seized evidence must be excluded, as a matter of due process, in the prosecution of accused persons tried in state courts. In 1963 the justices vetoed state laws requiring recital of the Lord's Prayer and Bible reading in public schools. In all these cases the Court took the position that government action restricting or taking away fundamental rights should be examined with special diligence, that "the Judiciary has the duty of implementing the constitutional safeguards that protect individual rights."

Reacting sharply to the Court's increasing preoccupation with civil rights in an age when pressures multiply to diminish them, Justice Harlan pointedly cautioned against the "subtle capacity for serious mischief" contained in the view that "all deficiencies in our society which have failed of correction by other means should

39

find a cure in the courts." "The Constitution does not confer on the Court," Harlan challenged on February 17, 1964, "blanket authority to step into every situation where the political branch may be thought to have fallen short." The Justice's concern is well taken. Surely no society can depend exclusively on the judiciary to safeguard it from harm. But, if the political process itself is impeded or corrupted, it would seem unrealistic to look to agencies which assume no responsibility for the breakdown as the sole organs of government empowered to furnish a corrective. Unless the judiciary intervenes, no remedy will be forthcoming.

Suspicion of an inconsistency between a nonelective, nonremovable, and potentially powerful Court, in a government deriving its powers from the consent of the governed, has always been of gnawing, tantalizing concern to Americans. It is still relevant to ask whether a politically nonresponsible body, such as the Supreme Court, can block the will of the majority in the name of minorities and remain a democratic institution. When the minority rights protected are those of property, the answer is probably *no*. Between 1890 and 1937, the Supreme Court in doing so retarded the growth of democracy. When, on the other hand, judicial review serves to give a minority (or a majority), otherwise barred, access to the political process, it implements rather than limits free government. The Court's function is not to determine what decisions can be made by political processes, but to prevent the mechanism from breaking down. Under this theory the legislature can control wages and hours of workers; it cannot limit the right to vote with respect to race or color. Congress can regulate agricultural production; it cannot control the content of newspapers. The state can demand that children attend school; it cannot compel them to participate in ceremonies that violate their religious convictions. Judicial hands-off in economic matters is perfectly consistent with judicial activism to preserve the integrity and effective operation of the political process.

The Supreme Court is a palladium of freedom. "Whether by force of circumstances or deliberate design," Americans have, as Woodrow Wilson put it, "married legislation with adjudication and look for statesmanship in Courts." With us all political issues ultimately resolve themselves into judicial questions.

"A great man," Justice Holmes once said of John Marshall, "represents a great ganglion in the nerves of society, . . . a strategic point in the campaign of history, and a part of his greatness consists in his being *there*." The same thing may be said of the Supreme Court. At every stage and in every phase of our national development, the Supreme Court has been *there*. From 1790 to 1835, the Court helped to establish a truly national government when the dominant political forces were moving in precisely the opposite direction. The Court was at the storm center of the slavery controversy in a misguided attempt to settle that perplexing issue. In the long struggle to reconcile industrial absolutism and political democracy, the Court played a delaying action. Today, when the national focus has shifted from the protection of property, the Court has taken the lead as guardian of personal rights, thus vindicating our claim to leadership of the Free World.

Judicial decisions, based on reason and authority, have a moral force far exceeding that of the purse or sword. What Walter Bagehot said of the English monarchy is, to some extent, true of the Supreme Court: it "strengthens our government with the strength of religion." The Court's firm command over the hearts and minds of Americans is not unrelated to the contemplative pause and the sober second thought its restraining power entails. The justices inform by both precept and example. They articulate and uphold the ideals and values that might otherwise be silenced. Far from discouraging civic responsibility, judicial decisions and Supreme Court opinions are among the greatest educational forces in America. In passing judgment on living issues, in resolving complexities which are at any given moment puzzling and dividing us, it teaches the demanding lesson of free government.

4 THE PRESIDENCY

Clinton Rossiter

The American Presidency is one of the few truly successful institutions created by men in the endless quest for
the blessings of free and stable government. The man
who holds this noble office enjoys a measure of authority
and prestige that is unique among all chief executives
in countries governed on constitutional principles. Who-
ever he may be, whatever may be his opinions, talents,
and personal qualities, he is inevitably one of the four or
five men to whom the world looks for guidance in the
long march to peace, freedom, and prosperity.

The Presidency, to be sure, is but one part of a complicated system of government. The Constitution of the
United States provides for three equal and independent
branches—the Congress (consisting of the Senate and
House of Representatives) to make laws, the President
to execute them, and the Supreme Court to interpret and
enforce them—and most legislators, all judges, and even
many administrators go about their tasks with little or
no thought about the President or his policies. The
authority of the government of the United States is
divided and limited to an extent unmatched in any other
country. There are many things the President can do
only with the cooperation of Congress and approval of
the Supreme Court; there are many things he cannot do

at all. Most important, he has no control over the procedures and decisions of Congress, the Supreme Court,
or the fifty state governments.

Nevertheless, the President is the central figure in the
American system, and any attempt to understand how
the United States is governed today must begin with an
account of his responsibilities. Let us consider briefly
some of the imposing tasks he is called upon to perform
by the Constitution, the laws, and custom.

The President is Chief Executive, the official charged
with supervising the activities of the two and one-third
million Americans in the national administration. He is
commanded by the Constitution to "take care that the
laws be faithfully executed." He is mandated by the
laws to prepare the government's annual budget, to set
rules for the civil service, and to encourage efficient
administrative practices. Most important, the people of
the United States expect him to see that honesty, efficiency, loyalty, and frugality prevail throughout the administration.

The Constitution designates the President specifically
as "Commander-in-Chief of the Army and Navy of the
United States." In peace and war he is, in fact, the un-
challenged, indeed unchallengeable, director of the
armed might of the nation. In time of peace he raises,
trains, supervises, and deploys the forces that Congress
is willing to maintain, and he has a great deal to say
about the size and make-up of these forces. In time of
war, he makes all major decisions of strategy (and many
of tactics as well), mobilizes the economy for maximum
production of the weapons of victory, and draws on the
memorable example of Abraham Lincoln to institute
measures that cut deeply into the lives of the people. As
the living guarantee of the American belief in the su-

premacy of civil over military authority, the President has a clear right to appoint and, if necessary, discharge all makers of policy in the defense department.

The President is also the leading figure in American diplomacy. Although authority in the field of foreign relations is divided among three organs—the President, Congress as a whole, and, for the approval of treaties and diplomatic appointments, the Senate—his claim to ascendancy is now acknowledged by most Americans in or out of the government. Congress is, as the world knows, an important partner of the President in the making of foreign policy. But on the whole, Congress is the sort of partner that criticizes rather than takes the lead itself. Secrecy, dispatch, unity, continuity, and access to information—the ingredients of successful diplomacy—are properties of the President's office, and Congress, an open forum of conflicting interests and opinions, possesses none of them. The Secretary of State, it should be noted, is subject directly to the President's orders, and holds office at the President's pleasure.

The President's duties are not all purely executive in nature. He is also closely associated with the work of Congress. The Constitution asks him to recommend to Congress "such measures as he shall judge necessary and expedient," and it grants him a qualified power of veto. Whenever he considers a bill passed by Congress to be unwise or unworkable or unconstitutional, he may return it without his signature. The bill cannot then become the law of the land unless it is passed again by a two-thirds majority in each of the two houses of Congress. In an ordinary year the President may exercise this power twenty-five or thirty times, and only occasionally does Congress go ahead to override his veto.

The President also exercises leadership of Congress by law and custom. Congress itself has sought leadership in such statutes as the Budget and Accounting Act of 1921, which requests the President to propose a detailed budget each year. Even more important, the people of the United States now expect their President to have a full program and to do his best to persuade Congress to enact it. Congress, of course, is not always easily persuaded. It is every bit as proud and independent as the President; it is one of the few legislatures in the world that cannot be dissolved for any reason. As a result, one of the interesting features of American political life is the occasional clash of personalities between a strong-minded President and strong-minded congressmen, especially senators of the opposing party.

The pressures of history have added at least four subsidiary but highly influential tasks to this strictly constitutional burden of the President: (1) The leadership of his party, which makes it possible for him to achieve a reasonably cohesive administration and also to make the appeal of party loyalty to roughly half the members of Congress. (2) The shaping and voicing of public opinion, of what Woodrow Wilson called "the real sentiment and purpose of the country." (3) The many-sided function of acting as the grand protector of "the peace of the United States," under which he can muster troops, experts, food, money, loans, equipment, medical supplies, and moral support to rescue Americans stricken by natural or social disaster. (4) The management (within the limits imposed by the practices and ideals of the American system of free enterprise) of the national economy, a task that calls upon him to take the lead in wielding what President Eisenhower described as the "formidable arsenal of weapons" now at "the disposal" of the national government for "maintaining economic stability."

When one puts these presidential roles together, then particularizes all this responsibility in terms of the constitutional authority to command, negotiate, veto, appoint, remove, pardon, and supervise as well as in terms of the statutory authority to make budgets, reduce tariffs, borrow money, close banks, and cool off strikes, one must conclude that never in history have free men put so much power in a single office. This is, indeed, a remarkable display of confidence in the good intentions of one man, a display rendered all the more remarkable because the man enjoys a kind of prestige that is unique among elected heads of government. The American Presidency unites the duties of two men in one office. In most countries two officials share the executive burden —the king or president or governor-general, who is the ceremonial head of state, and the prime minister or premier, who is the working head of government. In the United States the President is the working head and the "figurehead" as well. A great deal of his time is spent making proclamations to the people, holding state dinners and receptions, greeting distinguished visitors, and welcoming delegations of American citizens from all parts of the country and all walks of life. Although his position as symbol of the sovereignty and majesty of the American people adds to his huge burden of responsibility, it also adds to his prestige—and thus to his power. The framers of the Constitution, who may not have been quite sure what they were doing, took a momentous step when they blended the dignity of a king and the authority of a prime minister in one elective office.

Since the Constitution of the United States was written in 1787, the government has undergone very few structural changes. Indeed, in its main outlines this government is probably the oldest and most stable in the world. The changes that have taken place have been in emphasis rather than in form; most changes have been the result of unplanned growth rather than of conscious decision.

Perhaps the most visible change has been the evolution of the original Presidency to the mighty office I have just described. This evolution has not been steady; it has been subject to sharp ebbs as well as to massive flows. Strong Presidents have often been followed by weak ones; in the aftermath of every active Presidency, Congress has reasserted its own independence and power. Yet the ebbs have been more apparent than real, and each new strong President seems to have picked up where the last strong President left off. The course of the Presidency runs forcefully if discontinuously upward.

Why should the Presidency have developed into so powerful an office? Why has it outstripped both Congress and the Supreme Court in the typically American contest for authority and prestige?

The search for an answer to these interesting questions must begin with the Constitution itself. The Convention of 1787 met in Philadelphia at a time when most Americans, remembering the colonial years before the Revolution of 1776, had a sharp mistrust of executive power. For them the ideal form of government was a one-chambered assembly of the people's representatives to which a plural executive would be a mere appendage. Yet a small group of men, one of whom was a future President, James Madison of Virginia, campaigned tirelessly for an executive in the new Constitution who would have enough power and independence to counterbalance the legislature.

In the end, these men proved remarkably successful. Article II of the Constitution created the outlines of the office as its exists today. The most important decisions were those to make the executive power separate from the legislature, to place this power in the hands of one man, to give him a source of election outside the legislature, to grant him a fixed term of office and indefinite re-eligibility, and to bestow upon him the powers of ceremony, command, diplomacy, and administration, as well as qualified veto on the acts of Congress. Once Article II of the Constitution had been written and approved, and tested in the early years, the Presidency was on its way to the stature it enjoys today.

The search for an answer to my questions about the growth of the Presidency leads next to a survey of the entire sweep of American history. Among the circumstances that are usually credited with contributing to this growth are the increase in the size of the national administration in response to the challenges of a great industrial civilization, the deep involvement of the United States in foreign affairs, the three wars fought for American liberty since 1861, and such emergencies as the Pullman Strike of 1894 and the Depression of 1933. It is a fact of political science that great emergencies in the life of a constitutional democracy bring an increase in executive power and prestige, always at least temporarily, more often than not permanently; and Presidents like Abraham Lincoln, Woodrow Wilson, and Franklin D. Roosevelt left the office a stronger instrument because of the extraordinary actions they were forced to take in times of crisis.

Congress has contributed its bit to the rise of the Presidency. It now looks to the President for leadership as it certainly did not do before 1900. In addition, it cannot exercise its own authority without, in turn, increasing that of the President. Every time Congress passes a law to deal with some new problem of American life the President gains a new responsibility.

Finally, the Presidency has gathered strength and prestige from the steady rise of American democracy, especially of popular participation in the political process. For more than a century this office has been regarded by the American people as their special instrument and representative. If Congress represents the people as a collection of sections and interests, the President represents them as a nation. The Presidency depends directly on the people for much of its power and prestige, and it could shrink to a much lesser office if it should ever lose their support. It is, in any case, a matter of great importance that the President alone (and with him the Vice-President) is elected by the entire people of the United States.

The search leads in the end to the thirty-six Presidents themselves. None of these vast events—the rise of American industry, the entrance of America into world affairs, the crises of war and depression, the difficulties and exertions of Congress, or the triumph of democracy—could have had such influence on the Presidency if dedicated, talented men had not come to this high office and shaped events to their purposes. The Presidents, too, helped to build the Presidency, and so let us comment briefly on those whom American historians consider to have been the ablest and most influential.

The first of these was George Washington (1789–1797), who was, it is agreed, the best of all possible Presidents. Washington, a Virginia farmer who had commanded the victorious armies in the American Revolution, was the most celebrated and trusted man of his time. By lending his prestige to the new Republic, he won it a place among the nations of the earth. By acting decisively on a dozen or more occasions, he brought strength and independence to the untested Presidency. And by honoring scrupulously the new Constitution and the independent positions of Congress, the

Supreme Court, and the states, he struck a powerful blow for constitutional government. His voluntary retirement to his farm at the end of eight years in the Presidency was one of the critical events in the history of American freedom.

Thomas Jefferson, who served as third President between 1801 and 1809, is rightly considered the spokesman and symbol of American democracy. Today Americans of all parties and opinions appeal to his words and memory for support; many a politician would ask no more exalted title than to be known as a "Jeffersonian." Jefferson's memorable achievements as President were his founding of the Democratic party, his skillful use of this party to exert leadership over Congress, his bold decision to purchase the vast Louisiana Territory from Napoleon I in 1803, and his efforts to bring democratic simplicity to the national government. Jefferson was a greater man than he was a President, but certainly he ranks among the most influential men to have held the nation's highest office.

The seventh President, Andrew Jackson (1829–1837), was the first to be elected from one of the new states west of the Appalachian Mountains. The victory of Jackson, a farmer-soldier from Tennessee who had achieved widespread fame in the Battle of New Orleans (1814), was a protest against the domination of the national government by the older states along the Atlantic seaboard. Jackson's understanding of the art of government was crude and often misleading. But he did understand one fact clearly—that the Presidency had been grievously weakened during the years between 1809 and 1829 by the encroachment of Congress on its legitimate sphere— and he set out boldly to reassert the independence of the Executive. It was Jackson who first used the power of the veto with force and effect. Perhaps his most important contribution was to convince the American people that the Presidency was a democratic rather than an aristocratic instrument of government.

The most beloved of all American heroes, Abraham Lincoln of Illinois, was also one of the most successful American Presidents. During his Presidency (1861–1865), indeed because of his election, eleven southern states attempted to withdraw from the Union and set up a government of their own. Lincoln, like Jackson, had come to the Presidency from the pioneering West with little preparation and no clear understanding of his powers and duties. But, again like Jackson, he was obsessed with one grand idea: The Union must be preserved, by force if necessary. Through four terrible years Lincoln exhorted the people and directed the armies of the loyal states. The war was a bloody and bitter one, as only civil wars can be, yet Lincoln never lost his sense of compassion for those who suffered in the South as well as in the Union. A humble man, he was never corrupted by the power he wielded as Commander-in-Chief. He, like Washington, was first of all a believer in constitutional government.

It is probably still too early to predict enduring greatness for the Presidents of this century, but four seem destined to join Washington, Jefferson, Jackson, and Lincoln. Theodore Roosevelt of New York (1901–1909), a man of immense charm and vitality who appealed to the American people's delight in strenuous living and their concern for public morality; Woodrow Wilson of New Jersey (1913–1921), whose appearance at the Peace Conference in Paris in 1918 heralded a new role for America in the world; Franklin D. Roosevelt of New York (1933–1945), a strong President who rose enthusiastically to two demanding occasions, the Great Depression and World War II; and Harry S Truman of Missouri (1945–1953), who overcame a visible lack of preparation for the position and went on to become one of the most forceful Presidents in American history.

One point should be made quite clear about the Presidency of the United States: It is an office of great power; it is also an office whose power must be used within the limits of a complicated constitutional and political system designed primarily to preserve the liberties of the people for whom it exists. The limits upon the Presidency are many, and they have a way of exerting themselves even in time of desperate crisis. No significant national policy can be made effective without the approval of Congress, which retains in undiminished measure the power to pass laws and to appropriate money, as well as to investigate the activities of the President's lieutenants. No openly unconstitutional actions can escape the final censure of the Supreme Court. The opposing party, the free and active press, the permanent civil service, the governments of the fifty states, the giant corporations, labor unions, and foundations—all these independent centers of power can frustrate any President who attempts to overstep the boundaries of his rightful authority. Most important, no President, however admired, can now be elected for more than eight years. The precedent set voluntarily by Washington long ago has recently been fixed in the Constitution. Finally, a President may be impeached by the House of Representatives and removed from office by a two-thirds vote of the Senate for "treason, bribery, or other high crimes and misdemeanors." No President has yet been punished in this extraordinary manner, principally because each and every President, whatever his shortcomings, has proved himself a servant of freedom. The Presidency is above all and before all an instrument of constitutional government.

In the end, of course, the restraints that hold a President in line are internal rather than external, and it is one of the true prides of the American people that no one of their Presidents has been a scoundrel or a tyrant. Every President's conscience, training, and sense of history have joined to halt him short of the kind of deed that would destroy his fame and his standing with the people. If the President of the United States knows anything of history or politics or administration, he knows that he can do great things in the American system only in ways that honor the unwritten rules of constitutionalism, democracy, personal liberty, and moral behavior. These constitute the essence of the American tradition, and Americans are confident that they will never elect a President who is not devoted to them. The final strength of the American Presidency lies in the fact that it is an office of freedom.

5 THE PRESIDENT'S OFFICE

Herman M. Somers

The preceding chapter explained that the Presidency of
the United States is an office of unique characteristics,
with no precise parallel in other lands. The problem of
staffing the Presidency, furnishing the President with the
organizational and personal facilities to perform his
multifold great responsibilities, follows from the nature
of the office and is, therefore, also unique.

The United States government is correctly designated
as a presidential system, not a parliamentary system or a
cabinet system, or any other term suggesting collective
executive responsibility. The executive in the United
States is unitary. Powers are indeed shared throughout
the government, but by separated institutions with dis-
tinct although overlapping authority. The President is
not a product or a member of the legislature (the Congress), although he has a great deal of legislative authority. The President and members of Congress are
elected, and serve their terms of office, independently of
each other. The Chief Executive carries on his functions
through an independent mandate and with separate
constitutional authority that inheres in him personally.

The authority of the executive branch of government
rests in the President. He appoints all his departmental
and agency heads and they derive their authority
through him. He is the only elected executive official.

No officer of the executive branch may be a member of Congress. (The Vice-President has a special dual role which need not concern us here.) There is no constitutional Cabinet in the United States. By tradition, this name has been conferred upon the group of officials who head the major departments. They meet as a group only at the pleasure of the President. Some Presidents have held frequent and regular meetings of the Cabinet; others have chosen to do so only infrequently. Some have sought collective advice from this body; others, like President Kennedy, have preferred to deal with their departmental heads individually or in smaller groups. There is no collective responsibility or authority in the Cabinet or in any other assembly of agency heads. Constitutional authority and responsibility for decisions belong to the President.

The job of the Presidency has, of course, grown in volume and significance with the growth of governmental functions and their importance. As is true in other nations, the government has had to play an increasingly active role in the stability and growth of the national economy. Since World War II, its involvement in international affairs and organizations and its attention to military security have been unprecedented. These problems of government are becoming increasingly interrelated and often inseparable. The accelerating complexity and magnitude of this trend are only inadequately suggested by the elevenfold increase in our annual federal government expenditures since the last pre-World War II year—now reaching $100 billion a year.

The President has become the focus of responsibility and decision-making in all aspects of government, even though this cannot be noted in our Constitution or laws. His office (together with that of his Vice-President) is the only nationally elective one; he is the only official all citizens can vote for or against. He is automatically the head of his national party. As national policy has become more intricate and more pressing, the President has inevitably emerged as the initiator of the legislative agenda for Congress. The spotlight of the nation and of the world is upon him constantly. The history books now make his name the title not only for the administration he headed but also for the period during which he held office. He has become the symbol for the national condition, for good or ill. The public holds the President accountable for the success or failure of the entire administration, including its legislative program, despite the great constitutional and institutional limitations upon his actual powers.

While the great central role the President has come to play in American life adds vastly to his influence and effectiveness, it also adds enormous operating burdens. More than fifty departments and agencies report directly to the President. There are hundreds of bureaus with a considerable degree of autonomy within the departments to which they are formally attached. The heads of departments and agencies have specialized spheres of interest and responsibility. They compete for the attention and the priorities of the President in favor of their own limited jurisdictions. Their administrative and policy responsibilities have become so great that their capacity to act as advisers to the President on matters outside their direct responsibilities is limited.

These executives are also accountable to Congress, or to committees of Congress that are not only completely independent of the President (and often even of the Congress as a whole), but whose views and demands often differ from the President's. Similarly, our perma-

nent civil service is also compartmentalized and specialized. We have no equivalent of a government-wide administrative class, but something more akin to a career
service for each department.

Such forces exercise powerful centrifugal pulls upon
our government. The Constitution, with its principle of
separation of powers and its federal structure, and the
influences of a highly diversified social, economic, and
ethnic society of continental dimensions have resulted in
strong tendencies of separatism among the parts of the
government. It is a pluralistic government reflecting a
pluralistic nation.

Although such diversity holds strong assets for a
democratic nation, the pluralism has to be disciplined
so that government does not become paralyzed or cha-
otic. Within this decentralized pattern the Presidency
has come to be recognized as the great unifying force in
government and in the nation. The steady growth of
the President's influence in this century has been an
inescapable consequence of the growing size, complexity,
and importance of government. The increasing number
of important decisions that must be made—and only he
can make; the progressively more critical character of
such decisions—often bearing life and death implications not only for this country but also for much of the
world; and the frequent need that decisions be made
rapidly and enunciated by an identifiable, responsible
single voice have force unprecedented burdens on the
Presidency as the vital center of action and decision for
the entire government. Somehow the President must
pull together, coordinate, mesh, and control the vast and
agglomerate government.

It was long ago recognized that no individual alone
could conceivably manage such immense burdens.
Clearly the assistance a President requires could not

come exclusively from officials with specialized responsibilities and segmented outlooks. The President needs tools to oversee and harmonize the activities of the dispersed departments and agencies, in order to minimize the built-in tendency for departments to pursue independent courses of action, and to keep them in concert with his own goals. A President must, therefore, in this era be equipped with staff machinery which is detached from departmental and specialized interests, whose outlook and concerns are as government-wide as his own, which can act as an extension of the President himself, reflecting his responsibilities, his perceptions, and his priorities. Recognition of this necessity has resulted in the gradual development of an impressive administrative apparatus within the President's Office, which is officially designated as the Executive Office of the President.

The Executive Office was formally created in 1939, but of course various steps in that direction had been taken earlier. This was, however, the first time that Congress had authorized a staff organization directly within the President's Office. It followed upon a historic report prepared by the President's Committee on Administrative Management—independent scholars and experts who were asked to study the problems of managing the burgeoning government—whose detailed analyses and recommendations were aptly summarized in its appeal, "The President Needs Help."

The composition of the Executive Office has changed many times during the quarter-century of its existence. Some units have disappeared; new ones have been created. This process undoubtedly will continue with changes of circumstances and change of Presidents. The main outlines of the structure, however, have remained fairly constant. The units of the Executive Office fall into two general categories: (1) an intimate personal Presidential staff, called the White House Office; (2) several institutional units with more formal and regularized functions. Unlike the White House Office, the institutional units are, with the exception of their chiefs, generally staffed by career civil servants who go on from administration to administration.

It must be pointed out that the organization and administrative conduct of the Executive Office are inevitably a product of the particular personality, style, work habits, and predicament of the current President. No manuals or charts can be designed which will have constant relevance or utility for the Office as such. Of necessity, each President will arrange and use his Office in accordance with his own perception of the Presidency— which has varied widely among Presidents—and in the manner he finds most congenial. He has the flexibility to do so.

At present, the main institutional units in the Executive Office are the Bureau of the Budget, the Council of Economic Advisers, the National Security Council (to which is attached the Central Intelligence Agency), the Office of Space and Technology, the Office of Emergency Planning, and a National Aeronautics and Space Council. These are statutory units. From time to time the President may establish, by his own order, special units for specific tasks. Currently, one such organization is the Office of the Special Representative for Trade Negotiations, which is to advise and assist the President with respect to international commodity agreements, barriers to international trade, and the carrying out of our trade agreement program.

The permanent core of the institutional staff is the Bureau of the Budget, created in 1921, before there was an Executive Office, to enable the President to discharge the responsibilities of a manager with regard to the expenditures of the administrative agencies. Previously, each department of government had submitted, and defended, its budget directly to Congress. Thereafter, the President was made responsible for sending to Congress a consolidated financial program for the government, and he was equipped with a central agency for budgetary and administrative management. In performing these services for the President, the Bureau also renders an essential service to Congress, which has final responsibility for appropriating the funds and is empowered to make any upward or downward revisions in the Executive's proposals.

I presume that in every country the budgetary process is recognized as a major instrument of the Executive for translating policy into action processes and for controlling the activities of the several executive departments in accord with national policy, as well as for permitting orderly financial management. As budgetary decisions are often a major source of policy decisions, the budget becomes an instrument for planning. During the Kennedy administration, for example, each agency was obliged to submit its annual budget together with a five-year projection, program by program and year by year. Every existing, proposed, and anticipated program had to be priced out in advance. Thus, each agency was required to do considerable advance planning and examine more carefully its internal operations and controls. For the President it painted on a broad canvas the longer-range implications of this year's decisions and enlarged the base of knowledge for his choices and priorities.

The Bureau has many other important functions, one of which is to serve as a clearing house and coordinator for legislative policy for the entire executive branch.

Proposals emanating from departments or on which departments are expected to testify before Congress are submitted to the Bureau, which checks with all other affected agencies and indicates whether the position of the agency is in accord with the President's program. Thus the Budget Director is a key policy officer. He is obliged to see the President almost daily. He is a personal appointee of the President and serves at his pleasure; his appointment, unlike those of other heads of executive agencies, does not require Senate confirmation.

The Council of Economic Advisers was created in 1946 when the Congress enacted a formal policy for the government "to use all practicable means . . . to promote maximum employment, production, and purchasing power." The Council was conceived to be the study and planning instrument to effect this economic policy. It is composed of three members appointed by the President, who are assisted by a staff of career civil servants. Its formal functions are to carry on continuing analyses of the national economy, to advise the President on economic developments and problems, to appraise the economic policies of government, and to make recommendations to the President. It assists the President in the preparations of his annual economic report to the Congress.

The influence and use of the Council have varied greatly with different administrations. In the Kennedy administration, the Chairman of the Council became an intimate and conspicuous member of the President's personal group of advisers. He played a key role in both the development and advancement of the President's economic program. Thus far, President Johnson is using the Chairman in similar fashion. But, as was shown in some previous periods, it is possible for the Council to become little more than a relatively isolated study group.

The National Security Council is a different instrument. It is really an advisory committee composed of the Vice-President, the Secretaries of State and Defense, and the Director of the Office of Emergency Planning, with the President as chairman. It was established by law shortly after World War II to advise the President with respect to the integration of domestic, foreign, and military policies relating to national security. Presumably the Congress wanted to be sure there was formal machinery to regularize consultation among the major national security agencies and between them and the President.

During President Eisenhower's regime, the NSC developed into an elaborate machinery of interdepartmental committees for national security planning and for following up actions of departments in conformance with the decisions taken in the Council. Most prominent were the Planning Board and the Operations Coordinating Board. The effectiveness of such committees came under severe congressional criticism.

President Kennedy preferred to operate differently. He undertook to maximize control in his own hands and in his immediate staff. He distrusted collective decision-making and the diluting influence on information and decisions of formal permanent committees. He disliked having an unnecessary layer of interdepartmental committees between himself and his department heads. Consequently, he abolished the Operations Coordinating Board and the Planning Board. He transferred most of their responsibilities to individual department heads, so that accountability was always in an identifiable person rather than in a committee. He also erased the distinction between planning and operations, which he deemed to be one continual interactive process. Specific planning was assigned to the departments which would have to execute the plans. At the NSC staff level, broader planning and operational follow-up were merged in the same personnel. When an especially difficult interdepartmental problem arose, an ad hoc task force with a responsible head was created.

The NSC as a body declined in significance during the Kennedy regime. Formal meetings were seldom held. Many problems that had flowed routinely to weekly meetings were now handled by individual members meeting with the President or by memorandums, or at levels below the President. The President felt he could get better advice by dealing bilaterally or with small, informed groups than with committees of fixed membership and fixed meeting times. This was also the procedure he employed in dealing with his Cabinet. In short, Mr. Kennedy converted the formal interdepartmental committee machinery of the NSC into a direct working instrument of the President's Office and he restored direct communication, action, and policy flows between himself and the department heads. Thus the individual members of NSC, in their capacity as department heads, were given increased responsibility.

The Office of Science and Technology was created in the Executive Office in 1962. It was an outgrowth of the dramatic spurt in scientific and domestic policies. The OST has the job of coordinating and developing increasingly important, and controversial, science policy that transcends agency lines. It advises the President on methods to assure that science and technology are used most effectively in the interests of national security and the general welfare. There is also a Federal Council for Science and Technology, composed of the highest scientific officers in the principal research and development agencies. The Director of the Office serves as its chairman. He also serves as the President's special assistant and adviser for scientific affairs in the White House Office.

The Office of Emergency Planning is somewhat of a catchall agency. It advises and assists the President in determining and conducting policy for all emergency preparedness activities including the civil defense program, organization and continuity of government under emergency conditions, telecommunications management, and the planning of stockpiling of critical materials. In the emergency caused by the disastrous earthquake in Alaska, for example, the Director of the Office took charge of recovery operations. This office can be extremely important as a nucleus to enable the President to create agencies quickly required in emergency conditions. During World War II, President Roosevelt created most of the major agencies for mobilizing and regulating the war economy within the formal framework of the Office of Emergency Management, a predecessor of the present organization.

The National Aeronautics and Space Council is composed of the heads of four major departments and agencies, under the chairmanship of the Vice-President, to advise and assist the President on policies and plans for a comprehensive program in aeronautic and space activities. Its presence in the Executive Office is largely a formality, giving recognition to the new and staggering dimensions of the challenge in this field.

The White House Office is in no sense institutionalized or circumscribed. It consists of the President's personal aides, who most frequently carry the nondescriptive title of special assistant to the President. It is difficult to describe specifically the functions of this group of men. The *U.S. Government Manual* says simply, "The various Assistants to the President are personal aides and assist the President in such matters as he may direct." It adds, "The staff of the President facilitates and maintains communication with the Congress . . . the heads of executive departments and agencies, the press and other information media and the general public." In short, these men are eyes, ears, monitors, and advisers for the President, an extension of himself in his multifold responsibilities, to the degree and in the manner he finds most effective for his purposes.

President Eisenhower organized his White House staff in a hierarchical structure, probably reflecting his military background. He had a chief of staff known as Assistant to the President, who served as a central point of clearance for information and determined what required the President's attention. President Kennedy preferred informality and loose organization in his own office. He abolished the position of Assistant to the President and was his own chief of staff. He reduced the size of the staff to maximize direct access and to minimize any barriers that stand between himself and the heads of his departments. He was determined to avoid the dangers of isolation which threaten all Presidents. He wanted maximum direct exposure to information and ideas and criticism from a variety of sources, both within and outside the government. He encouraged an informal arrangement that permitted even officers in sub-Cabinet levels, or lower, to bypass their superiors and reach the President when they felt it necessary.

His staff was arranged in small clusters of three or four men with one recognized as the central figure. Work areas were not sharply demarcated but extremely fluid and changing. Almost all the men were broad generalists who could readily be moved from one assignment to another. Kennedy felt that his Office was not an appropriate place for specialists but rather for broadly educated intelligent men who could, with the same broad perspective and interest as his own, get on top of the varied problems that face a President. For the most part, the groups were organized around action-enforcing processes rather than special program areas.

Some assignments were, by their nature, more clearly defined than others—such as the President's press secretary and his appointments secretary. But the President's special counsel headed a group concerned with the entire range of domestic issues, preparation of speeches and messages, and just about everything calling for a President's attention that somebody else was not handling. The Special Assistant for National Security Affairs was primarily concerned with the gamut of international and national security problems, but he was also interested in their domestic implications. One man headed a group dealing with congressional relations. There was also the President's science adviser. Others had ad hoc assignments in foreign economic aid or civil liberties and other problems as the situation required. All of them had to be ready, however, to serve interchangeably as the flow of action and the President demanded. The President dealt with them individually or in small groups, but they all had direct access to him. He frequently established ad hoc task forces for special problems on which he combined members of his own staff with department or agency heads. At all times, Mr. Kennedy wanted to be sure that he was not cut off from a diversity of views and alternatives. He also minimized the distinction between his personal staff and the heads of institutional agencies of the Executive Office, particularly in the case of the Director of the Budget and the Chairman of the Council on Economic Advisers, and he used them as intermingled with his White House Office.

The job of the President's Office, when properly utilized, is to keep the President fully informed, to help him monitor the departments and agencies, to help develop his program, to bring him early warning of items for his agenda before his options are foreclosed, to help him lift out of the cumbersome normal channels of big government those items he chooses to make his priorities, to help him obtain priority attention from key officials on the items he elevates to his own level. The Office offers the President the administrative means to be head of the government in fact as well as in name.

Ultimately the government must speak with a single voice. It is at the President's desk that the vast complex of government problems and their diverse considerations, touching many conflicting interests of a large nation and often many other parts of the world, finally converge and must somehow be joined and reconciled. In the nuclear age the daily decisions, both large and small, of the President of the United States have assumed a new dimension of risk and importance. The small decisions cannot be ignored; in today's world they are often irreversible in their effects and can predetermine the large ones. More than ever, therefore, the reality of responsible democratic government depends on the ability of the President to control the decisions and activities of the executive branch.

The President's Office has proved to be an essential and practical organizational facility. Of course, it guarantees nothing in itself. Its effective use must ultimately depend on the vitality, the style, and the wisdom of the President.

6 THE UNITED STATES CONGRESS

James MacGregor Burns

Exciting and revolutionary ideas swept the Western world during the late eighteenth century. One of these was that people could govern themselves, that they could dispense with monarchs, dictators, oligarchs, or tyrants and run their own affairs through their own representatives. The institutional form of this idea was the Congress—a body of locally elected or appointed men who would assemble in a central place, deliberate freely without interference from kings or other authority, and frame wise and benevolent laws for the good of the people.

This idea lay behind the creation of the United States Congress as the central and positive branch of the government of the new United States. The framers of the American Constitution, meeting in Philadelphia in 1787, were heirs to John Locke, who had emphasized majority rule and legislative supremacy, on the one hand, and limited government, on the other. By the terms of Locke's social contract men promised to abide by the decisions of the majority; at the same time, government was limited to the purpose for which it was established. Whenever government became destructive of the inalienable rights of man, it could no longer claim his allegiance.

There was thus a central ambiguity in Locke. This ambiguity was passed on to early American thinkers and was reinforced by the doctrines of another philosopher who influenced the thought of the framers of the Constitution, Montesquieu. Like Locke, the great French theorist felt that liberty should be secured *against* government; moreover, he proposed a practical means of accomplishing this—the separation of powers. He proposed to check power with power, by giving some authority to the legislature, some to the executive, and some to the judiciary.

The practical experience of the framers fortified their interest in checking power with power. They had long resisted the power of the Crown, as manifested in the authority of royal governors and other "minions" of the King. The Revolution had in part been a form of resistance to executive authority, and the framers were of no mind to establish a strong new executive, even under a more democratic system of government. But they could not be complacent about legislative authority, for they had seen abuses and failings in this kind of power too. They also had mixed feelings about judicial authority. What better solution than to mix and blend governmental power among a host of competing leaders, each holding different powers, each responding to different electorates or constituencies? This was the basic design of the Constitution, and it represented one of the most brilliant and durable examples of political planning in history.

Underlying this theory of government was a theory of *man*—a theory that combined optimism over the power of the people and their representatives to govern wisely, and a deep skepticism, even cynicism, over the basically selfish and power-seeking qualities of man. The framers had imbibed Hume's skepticism and Machiavelli's cynicism and Hobbes's realism together with the teachings of Locke and Montesquieu. Their concern was far less to realize life, liberty, and happiness *through* government than to protect those great values *against* government.

The upshot in Philadelphia in 1787 was a new federal government of limited and divided powers—powers that were carefully circumscribed in order not to encroach on basic powers left to the states and to the people, with the remaining national power further parceled out to a Congress with two branches, to the President, and to the judicial branch. Congress was put in a rather ambivalent position; it was the central, law-making branch of the national government, but it was left in a competitive relation with a President of rather ambiguous powers but of enormous potential importance, and with a judiciary that was given implicitly the power to hold acts of Congress, as well as actions of the President, unconstitutional.

Still, Congress was to be the keystone of the federal government; in policy-making the President and the judiciary were to be more negative and specialized branches. The past century has witnessed an interesting reversal in emphasis. The Presidency has become an important source of initiative and planning, of policy and program, and the federal judiciary has made some historic decisions, especially in the field of civil rights. Congress has assumed some negative functions—vetoing proposals of the President, investigating activities of the executive department, and sometimes reducing appropriations requested by the Chief Executive. One reporter noted that Congress has become a kind of continuing and permanent opposition party to the President, any President. This, of course, is an overstatement—for on many notable public issues in such fields as national defense and foreign policy the Congress has acted with dispatch as an ally of presidential policies. But it is certainly true that on occasion Congress has moved into a position of critical challenge to executive-sponsored programs.

The historic causes of this reversal are manifold. First, most Presidents, beginning with George Washington, have insisted on protecting their executive prerogatives against attempts by Congress to exert administrative controls over at least sections of the bureaucracy. As the federal bureaucracy has become larger and grown into a vast apparatus, the executive reach of the President has naturally grown too. Second, to win and keep office presidential aspirants or incumbents had to build strong party followings and in doing so they both shaped and maintained a base of political power that sustained them in their altercations with Congress. Thomas Jefferson and Andrew Jackson exemplified this tendency. Third, the managing of warfare, hot or cold, has greatly enhanced the power of the President. Abraham Lincoln directed the Northern effort against the South for several months without even calling Congress into session. Woodrow Wilson and Franklin Roosevelt wielded extensive powers in directing American efforts in the two world wars, and much of the enhanced presidential authority continued, at least in the form of precedent and practice, following the termination of the wars.

The main reason for the reversal of the roles of President and Congress goes beyond even these significant factors. Put oversimply, the President as an institution has responded to the needs and pressures of a complex and growing urban population, while Congress—representing a more conservatively oriented and traditional series of constituencies—has not. There are three dimensions to this contrast.

In the first place, Congress does not fully represent the urban population, while the President may over-represent city dwellers. The Senate was established to give all states equal representation regardless of population, and this provision in effect has meant that the less populous rural states, such as Idaho and Vermont, have the same formal representation, two senators, in the upper chamber as do populous urban states like California and New York. This was to be expected and, indeed, was even part of the planning of the founding fathers. Much more surprising has been the shift in representation in the House of Representatives, which was designed to be directly representative of population, large or small. The House has become, many observers feel, even less responsive to urban interests than has the Senate.

There is a natural reason for this seeming paradox. Legislative district lines can never keep pace with the flow of population, even with the best of intentions, and since the flow of population has been essentially from country to city (and now into suburbs), political boundaries are always at least a little out of date. Together with this uncalculated malrepresentation, there has been a good deal of contrived maldistricting of congressional constituencies. The power to set the boundaries of congressional districts lies in effect with the state legislatures, which are themselves artificially constructed to overrepresent rural areas. Although they have the legal opportunity to redistrict at least every ten years, the state legislators are perfectly content to allow urban districts to become two or three times larger than rural ones; hence they greatly depreciate the representation of urban interests in the national House of Representatives. A recent Supreme Court decision requires that these gross disparities be changed, but it may be some time before

73

all congressional districts are evened up to meet the rough criteria established by the Court.

The Presidency must be far more responsive to urban interests because success in gaining the White House turns on capturing a majority of the electoral votes of the states, and the large states have almost their proportionate share of these votes. As a practical matter, the presidential candidates tend to vie for the great urban voting blocks, such as labor and ethnic groups, that are thought to hold the balance of power in the large states, and in doing so make promises and commitments that draw them even farther from the views and policies of congressmen who represent the rural districts.

A second reason for the change in the congressional role and the rise of presidential initiative is institutional. Part of the great strength of the Presidency has been the principle that Alexander Hamilton and other framers of the Constitution stressed at the start—the need for single authority, for unity of command, for concentration of power, at least within the executive branch. Congress has become increasingly characterized by multiple leadership and by organizational diversity.

On the face of it, Congress would seem to be organized on party lines, to be characterized by the same leadership of the "ins" and of the "outs" that is found in many other national legislatures, such as the British Parliament. Both the Senate and the House are organized, visibly as well as behind the scenes, in party groupings, with party labels; the majority party controls the committees and other key institutions and functions; there is the usual apparatus of party leaders, whips, and other traditional elements of party control. There is an opposition party "with the duty to oppose," and with its own minority party apparatus.

Behind this façade of a two-party system, however,

Congress is organized on a highly diffused and factional basis. It operates a multiparty rather than a two-party system. Power is divided between the elected leaders, such as the Speaker of the House and the majority leader of the Senate, on the one hand, and the committee leaders, on the other. The power of the committee leaders is further fragmented because of the multiplicity of committees and subcommittees in both houses. While the thrust of the Presidency is always toward the concentration of power, the drift of Congress is toward the scattering of power among a dozen or so key leaders and among perhaps another hundred secondary leaders.

The device that most effectively fragments congressional policy-making is the committee system combined with the seniority rule. The making of policy in Congress has traditionally been divided among standing committees, many of which have attained great prestige and influence. The Senate Finance Committee, the Senate Foreign Relations Committee, and the House Ways and Means (money-raising) Committee have been led by some of the ablest members of Congress, who have built long and notable careers out of their roles in these committees. Although committees cannot legislate on their own and must recommend measures to their parent chambers, their recommendations carry more than ordinary weight with the legislature as a whole because of a tendency toward mutual forbearance and protection among the stronger committees. This is especially the case with the appropriations committees.

Committee chairmanships are allotted on the basis of the famous congressional seniority rule—the man who has had the longest service on the committee becomes chairman, if he belongs to the majority party. Moreover, committee chairmen wield great powers—power to hold meetings or not hold them, power to advance some bills in the committee and to block others, power to influence the management of a committee measure if and when it reaches the floor of the House or Senate. The crucial question is: In whose hands do committee chairmenships tend to gravitate? The answer is quite clear from American experience; in general, those men from the more socially stable, conservative, rural areas are the congressmen who face least competition from the opposition party and hence stay in Congress and accumulate seniority and ultimately committee chairmanships. Factually, the conservative rural population of the nation—now far smaller than the urban and suburban population—is substantially overrepresented in the committee structure and thus in the policy-making of Congress.

Seniority is not simply a technical parliamentary rule in Congress; it is a way of life. Not only chairmanships but other political prizes and considerations usually are allotted on the basis of longest service in Congress. Even though committee chairmen do not work in close alliance with one another, they support a system of mutual toleration and mutual assistance. The younger legislator comes to feel that he must "go along" with his elders in order to "get along." He may be newly elected from an area of keen competition between the two parties; he may feel that he has a mandate from his constituency to propose strong action; he may wish to support a vigorous President who has proposed sweeping measures to Congress. But he also wants to move ahead in influence within the congressional structure, and a tension is often created between his desire to be bold and his prudent calculation that he must in part "play the game" according to both formal and informal congressional rules.

A third major reason for the change in congressional role is closely related to the seniority system; namely, the special arrangements in each house that make action difficult. If the executive branch is generally organized to expedite action, basically Congress is organized to slow up, consider, refine, and even block action. The rules of each house, especially the Senate, permit expert parliamentarians to delay or to block action in many ingenious ways, but two procedures in particular play into the hands of those who wish to slow the legislative process.

The most noted of these is the right to filibuster in the Senate. Once a senator gains the floor, he has the power to go on speaking until he gives up the floor voluntarily or through exhaustion. Debate does not have to be relevant to the subject under consideration; the senator need only keep talking. If several senators want to filibuster, they can do so by spelling one another hour after hour— for example, by asking involved questions that enable the speaker to rest. The only way to end a filibuster is by giving in to the filibusterers, by exhausting them (almost impossible), or by invoking cloture. If two-thirds of the senators on the floor vote for cloture, no senator may speak for more than an hour. The Senate has rarely invoked cloture, however, and the filibuster remains a formidable weapon of delay and obstruction in the Senate. In the next chapter, Joseph P. Harris will discuss the filibuster more fully, as well as its institutional counterpart in the House of Representatives, the Rules Committee. On the face of it, the Rules Committee is simply a "traffic officer" that does the vital job of regulating the flow of business to enable the more important bills to receive expeditious handling. Actually, the Committee has the power to delay a bill indefinitely and in effect kill it; to substitute a wholly new bill; or to insist that the bill be drastically amended as the price of letting it go on to the House floor. The Rules Committee also operates under the seniority rule and it is not a representative committee; it is dominated by veteran congress-

men who have been re-elected time and time again from
"safe" districts regardless of the shifts in national political alignments. In effect, a coalition of conservative
Republicans and conservative Democrats—most of them
from rural areas—has dominated the Rules Committee in
recent decades.

Clearly the hand of tradition lies heavily on the houses
of Congress—the hand of the framers, who built a congressional structure that remains little changed, in contrast to the tremendous alterations in both the form and
substance of the Presidency; and the hand of the older,
more conservative members from rural districts who
oppose vigorous federal action and use Congress essentially as a means of containing strong Presidents.

Can Congress, then, face up to the needs of a highly
complex, constantly changing, and increasingly urbanized America? One answer, of course, is that it *has* so
faced up on many occasions. The legislative record of the
past twenty years indicates some massive responses to the
great economic and social needs of urban America: social
security, fair labor standards, public housing and slum
clearance, collective bargaining, depositors insurance,
health, welfare, and educational grants—these are but
some of the laws passed by Congress to meet the changing
needs of American life.

Furthermore, the 89th Congress has moved swiftly in
weakening the power of the House Rules Committee to
obstruct legislation, thereby opening the way for full
House action on the President's program.

Many Americans, of course, *like* a sticky Congress; they
see in Congress a check on activist, majoritarian, inter-
nationalist, and what some would call "spendthrift" and
"radical" Presidents. They would contend that the more
Congress waters down and obstructs certain presidential
measures, the more it acts as an effective check and

balance in our pluralistic society against dangerous and radical majoritarian impulses in both domestic and international fields. The claim here is that we can move safely only if we move slowly.

Such people would oppose any fundamental congressional reform designed to make the national legislature more expeditious and innovative. They might well hold winning cards in any struggle over extensive reform, because many of the congressmen who reflect their views are the ones who hold the strategic positions from which they can deflect any reforms designed to change the operations of Congress. Committee chairmen and their friends can influence procedural reform bills just as they can bottle up substantive measures. The very procedures that reformers would wish to change—most notably the seniority system and the right to filibuster—are the very procedures that can be used to block such changes or to delay them inordinately.

Another strategy of reform is constitutional amendment. Reformers have favored proposals to elect members of the House of Representatives every four years, as at present; to limit the terms of senators to four years (probably an impossibility); to establish a joint presidential-legislative cabinet including members from both the executive and the legislative branches; and possibly even to give the President the power of dissolving Congress and compelling the members to run for re-election, in the manner of some parliamentary democracies abroad. Such reforms are probably overly ambitious and perhaps faulty in concept (for example, the right of dissolution); in any event, major reform of Congress through constitutional reform could hardly muster the two-thirds vote needed in both houses of Congress, or the necessary support of three-fourths of the state legislatures.

79

If this analysis is correct, what we end up with super-
ficially is another example of the irresistible force and
the immovable object. Certainly Congress is an intractable if not an immovable object in the area of self-
reform and a slow-moving object in enacting major social
and economic legislation. But if we should not minimize
the immovability of the object, we must not under-
estimate either the irresistibility of the force. The civil
rights movement in the United States has required
tremendous momentum. The crucial question is not
whether this force will continue to be exerted, but
whether it will be channeled through regular processes
of governmental action, or whether it will operate
mainly in the streets, at the lunch counters, in the
schools and universities. The current struggle over civil
rights legislation is a great testing of this question. We
must keep in mind that civil rights is merely one focus
of movements for social reform. Allied with it are those
policies concerned with the pockets of poverty in the
United States, the economy, education and training,
transportation, medical care for the aged, and the plight
of the cities, embracing a wide range of problems from
juvenile delinquency to air pollution. These forces themselves may move the Congress to more rapid and positive
action. If these forces of change and reform, seeking
stronger federal action, cannot find adequate relief and
representation in Congress, they will turn to another
agency that historically has been more responsive to the
urban, ethnic, racial, trade-union, and consumer-minded
population of the United States: the Presidency. Some of
the reformers' aims can be realized through direct presidential action. But the basic domestic issues facing the
United States are essentially fiscal; they concern the
allocation of resources to the public sector, and their re-
allocation to public needs, such as social welfare or de-

fense spending. It is in the allocation of resources to these public needs that the President is most helpless to act alone; here he must gain the consent of Congress. It is precisely here that Congress will be forced by events and by presidential leadership to consider anew the appropriate balance between economy, balancing the budget and "protecting the taxpayer's dollar" on the one hand; and the insistent demands of an increasingly complex and urbanized society on the other.

The existence of friction between the President and the Congress on these issues is not surprising; in part it is a result of the checks and balances that the framers of the Constitution established almost two hundred years ago. Most Americans, whatever their specific interests in policy, support the system of checks and balances and the limited government that it sustains. A change in the basic functions and thrust of Congress would call both for an act of creative imagination by political leaders, rivaling the boldness of the framers of the Constitution, and for a change in popular attitudes that sustain the present structure of government. The historic and continuing question is whether Congress can continue to protect our taxpayers' pocketbooks at the same time that it plays a positive and constructive role in helping the President to meet the unprecedented needs of mankind at home and abroad.

7 THE TWO HOUSES OF CONGRESS

Joseph P. Harris

Its members are fond of referring to Congress as "the greatest legislative body on earth." Whether it is the greatest can be disputed, but Congress is undoubtedly the most powerful legislative body in the world. With the great expansion of the federal government—which today has an annual budget of more than $100 billion, and more than two and one-half million employees—Congress passes on policies and programs that affect the economy not only of this country but also of the free world. Formerly members of Congress were concerned almost entirely with domestic issues and policies; today there are few major bills before Congress that do not have an impact on international as well as on national affairs.

At the end of World War II many informed people doubted that the President and the Congress would be able to work together effectively in determining the domestic and international policies required in the postwar period. The events since 1945 have not borne out these doubts and fears. Despite occasional conflicts between the President and the Congress, and the fact that during most of the period since the end of the war the President has been opposed by a majority of Congress (including bipartisan coalitions), the two branches of government have shown a remarkable degree of cooperation in international affairs. Their differences have been more marked in domestic affairs, where the government often has been unable to cope with pressing problems. Congress has adjusted its organization and procedures to meet its new and greater responsibilities. Additional reforms, however, are still needed. Since 1946 Congress has improved its committee system, strengthened its staff and procedures, enormously increased its expenditures for investigations, and is now far better equipped to act upon legislation and to watch over the administration.

The decision of the framers of the Constitution to establish a bicameral legislative body consisting of the House of Representatives and the Senate was one of the "great compromises" of the Convention. The smaller states, fearing that a single legislative body apportioned among the states on the basis of population would lead to its domination by a few of the larger states, were able to secure the creation of a second chamber in which each state, regardless of population, would have equal representation. The fears of the smaller states proved to be groundless; there has seldom, if ever, been a division in the House of Representatives in which the more populous states were aligned against the smaller states. But the system of representation that gives all states equal representation in the Senate is firmly established in the Constitution and cannot be changed without the consent of every state.

The framers of the Constitution feared that the lower house, being directly elected by the people and responsible to their demands, would be moved by popular passions and act hastily, violating the rights of property

83

owners and the well-to-do. They thought that the Senate, being a smaller body and composed of older persons selected by the state legislatures, would provide a check on radical legislation passed by the lower house. For the first hundred years the Senate was indeed the more conservative body. Because it was composed primarily of men of wealth, it was often called the "millionaires' club." Since the adoption in 1913 of the Seventeenth Amendment, which provided for popular election of senators, the Senate has often been more liberal than the House.

THE HOUSE OF REPRESENTATIVES

The number of members of the House of Representatives has been fixed at 435. Seats are apportioned to the fifty states on the basis of population after each decennial census. States with rapidly increasing populations, such as California, receive additional seats after each census, while states with stable populations suffer a loss. Members are elected, as a rule, from single-member districts. As a result, the majority political party often has more seats than it is entitled to on the basis of votes received. Proportional representation, although widely used in Europe, has not found favor in the United States.

As James M. Burns noted in the preceding chapter, each state legislature determines the boundaries of districts for the election of members of the House of Representatives. The state constitutions usually require the legislature to redistrict after each census, but this requirement is often disregarded. Rural-dominated state legislatures have generally been unwilling to accord seats in proportion to population of rapidly growing urban areas. Congressional districts are usually drawn to give a maximum number of seats to the majority party.

Districts with weird shapes are often created, a practice called "gerrymandering."

Although congressional districts are supposed to have approximately equal populations, because of partisanship, the struggle between rural and urban areas, and the failure of state legislatures to redistrict, the population of congressional districts varies widely. Many districts have less than 300,000, while other districts have more than double that population. Until recently the Supreme Court refused to intervene in the legislative redistricting, maintaining that it was a political decision to be made by the legislature, but in a series of decisions in recent years the Court has reversed itself and has held that legislative districts must not be grossly unequal in population.

Members of the House of Representatives are elected every two years. Hardly has the congressman arrived in Washington to take up his duties as a legislator before he must begin his campaign for re-election. The cost of primary and election campaigns is very high, especially in urban districts where the two parties are fairly evenly divided. In close contests it is not unusual for the campaign expenditures on behalf of the winning candidate to exceed $50,000, or almost as much as his entire salary during his term of office.

The nomination of candidates for Congress is strictly local; national and state party organizations usually have nothing to do with it. The nominee usually is chosen by the local party leaders and the party organization, to whom he feels heavily obligated. It is for this reason that members of Congress are influenced more by the wishes of local party leaders and their principal financial contributors than by national party leaders.

In order to gain support back home, members of Congress devote much time and energy to rendering a variety of services to their constituents. If a citizen wants some action from a department, such as a government contract, a son discharged from the armed services, a government job not under civil service, or if a veteran wants to appeal a decision affecting his pension and is unable to get desired action from the department, he turns to his congressman for assistance.

Congressmen, with the aid of chambers of commerce and other local organizations, spend a large part of their time seeking federal expenditures of benefit to their districts. Rivers and harbors that carry little traffic have been improved at large expense by the federal government because of the influence of local congressmen, who team up with other members of Congress who have similar projects in their districts.

Approximately 60 per cent of the members of both houses of Congress are attorneys. The reasons are obvious. Many persons who enter the legal profession are interested in politics and become candidates for public office when the occasion presents itself. Attorneys who are members of law firms are better able to combine public office with a professional career. The lawyer is well trained to serve as a legislator not only because he is familiar with statutes and court decisions but also because his training prepares him for becoming an advocate for people in all walks of life. Yet it would appear that Congress, as well as other legislative bodies, could benefit by having a more widely diversified representation from other professions and occupational groups.

The presiding officer of the House of Representatives has the title of Speaker. He is elected by each Congress, and by tradition the Speaker is the leader of the majority party. Formerly he enjoyed great powers and, together with a small group of assistants, he controlled the actions of the House. Fifty years ago, however, the Speaker was shorn of many of his powers; today he must exercise leadership largely by persuasion, rather than dictation.

The most powerful body in the House of Representatives is the Rules Committee, which selects the bills to be considered by the House. Bills recommended for passage by other committees must ordinarily secure a special rule from the Rules Committee before they can be taken up.

The customary procedure is for the chairman of a standing committee which has reported a bill to the House to apply to the Rules Committee for a special rule that will bring it up for consideration. Sometimes the Rules Committee conducts hearings on the merits of a pending bill, even though the standing committee has already conducted extended hearings, and it is not uncommon for the Rules Committee to require the bill to be revised before permitting it to be considered by the House.

Until the dramatic change in the power of the Rules Committee made at the opening of the 89th Congress, the refusal of the committee to report a special rule meant almost certain death to a proposed bill. The Rules Committee in recent years has blocked action on many important bills, including those on federal aid to education, minimum wages, urban affairs, civil rights, and others. The Rules Committee has long been dominated by conservative members of both political parties and has succeeded in blocking or delaying many liberal bills. Under the new provision, the Speaker may in effect call a bill from the Rules Committee's jurisdiction after twenty-one days. This is a significant change in House procedures. No longer will it be possible for the Rules Committee to prevent a bill's being taken up by the House when a majority of its members can convince the Speaker that they are ready to vote on it.

THE SENATE

The United States Senate is by all odds the most powerful upper chamber of any legislature in the world. Its legislative power equals that of the House of Representatives, which is generally not true of other upper chambers; in addition, it enjoys two great powers which it does not share with the House. Its power to approve or disapprove treaties with foreign countries and to confirm or reject nominations of ambassadors and the principal officers of the State Department gives it a preeminent place in foreign affairs. The President and the State Department maintain close contacts with the powerful Senate Committee on Foreign Relations, and they consult its members about important policies and relations with other countries before they are put into effect. The President's first consideration in choosing a Secretary of State is whether the person of his choice can get along with the leaders of the Senate. For this reason senators are often offered the post.

The power of the Senate to pass upon the President's nominations adds greatly to its authority as well as to the political patronage wielded by individual senators of the President's party. Under the unwritten rule of "senatorial courtesy," the Senate will reject a nominee who is objected to by a senator from the state where he is to serve. The effect of the rule is to transfer the power of nomination of federal field officers from the President to the senators of each state, provided they are members of the President's party. This gives the senators important patronage and is a symbol of power in their states. The requirement of confirmation gives the Senate a powerful sanction over the appointments of the President and a control over executive officers that is not enjoyed by the House of Representatives.

It has been said, not without exaggeration, that the Senate is the most exclusive club in the world. Only senators who abide by the customs of the Senate and are highly respected by their colleagues are accepted in the inner club, usually after a number of years of service. These are the senators of both political parties who virtually run the Senate.

A new member serves an apprenticeship when he enters the Senate. He receives committee assignments to the least important committees, and in the committee room he sits at the end of the table. During the first year he is expected to be seen but not heard. Senators who violate this rule incur the displeasure of their colleagues and may never be accepted in the inner circle. They are expected to show respect to their elders and to perform the boring tasks that other senators want to avoid. In order to gain the respect of their colleagues, they must specialize in certain areas of legislation, acquire the reputation of being a work horse, not a show horse, and conform to the customs and traditions of the Senate.

Political parties play a relatively minor role in the two houses of Congress, especially in comparison with European parliaments. Votes strictly on party lines are uncommon, although partisan considerations are seldom absent when Congress acts on important policies. The votes are usually dictated by state and local considerations rather than by national party policy. A strong President may be able to secure the support of members of his party on most of his legislative program, but he can never be sure of their votes, and often, as in the case of civil rights legislation, he must appeal for support from the opposition party. The organization and traditions of Congress place great power and independence in the hands of its senior members, who are subject to little national party control.

COMMITTEE SYSTEM

The real work of Congress is transacted not on the floor of the two chambers but in the committees, which have been called "little legislatures." Because of the increase in the number and importance of the standing subcommittees, since 1946, it is more accurate to say that today the real work of Congress is transacted by the subcommittees. Congress utilizes committees and subcommittees more than any other legislative body in the world; it grants them greater powers and exercises less control over them than do other legislative bodies.

The Senate has sixteen standing committees and the House has twenty. With one or two exceptions, these standing committees are assigned specified areas of legislation. Thus, each house has committees on foreign relations, appropriations, revenues, armed services, agriculture, judiciary, commerce, and labor. In a few fields such as atomic energy, internal revenue taxation, and the President's economic report, Congress has established joint committees with members drawn from both houses. These joint committees must not be confused, however, with conference committees.

Conference committees are established when the House and Senate fail to agree on the provisions of a bill. Most important bills are sent to conference committees, which consist of the ranking members in both parties of the standing committees that reported the bill. The conference committees, which meet in closed sessions, wield a great deal of power. They often make substantial changes in bills, although under the rules they are not permitted to introduce new provisions except to compromise the differences in the bill as it passed the two houses.

Every member of Congress seeks assignment to one of the major committees, especially the "bread-and-butter" committees whose activities relate to his own district or state. Western congressmen often seek assignment to the Interior or Public Works Committees, which pass upon public works projects and programs of interest to the West; those from agricultural areas want to be assigned to the Agriculture Committee; others seek an assignment to the Appropriations Committee, because of its great power, or to the Rules Committee of the House. The Foreign Relations Committee of the Senate ranks first in member preference in the Senate, followed in order by the Appropriations, Finance, Armed Services, and Agriculture Committees. Committee preference in the House is similar to that in the Senate. The two committees that rank lowest in membership preference in each house are those on the District of Columbia and the Post Office and Civil Service.

Chairmen of standing committees are the real leaders of Congress, although their powers have declined with the increasing use of subcommittees. The chairman is invariably the ranking member of the majority party in length of service on the committee and is usually highly respected by his colleagues. Because of his prestige and the great power that he wields, he is usually able to control the actions of the committee. Some chairmen rule with an iron hand, even refusing to permit consideration of bills to which they are opposed, but most chairmen act in a more democratic and responsible manner.

Most committee chairmen have served ten or more years on the committee and through long and continual service they have acquired a great deal of knowledge about the legislation within its jurisdiction. They become informed about major bills before the committee, and can turn to the committee staff for research or assistance. Although at times the chairman is overruled by the committee, such cases are rare. Members of the committee, who may later seek favors that only the chairman can grant, are reluctant to oppose his wishes.

Because of their extraordinary power, committee chairmen are cultivated by the President, the press, pressure groups, executive departments, and, of course, by other senators and congressmen. A speech by the chairman of an important congressional committee generally has news value across the nation and often around the world. Especially in the field of foreign affairs, the chairmen of the Senate Foreign Relations Committee and the House Foreign Affairs Committee are watched attentively by the chanceries of a hundred nations across the face of the globe. Foreign observers are also closely attuned to the attitudes and activities of powerful subcommittee chairmen in the appropriations committees of the two houses. These subcommittee chairmen often possess enormous personal power over the fate of appropriations for economic and military aid abroad—matters of no small moment to recipient countries.

LEGISLATIVE PROCESS IN CONGRESS

Fifteen thousand bills are introduced every two years, but less than one thousand ever emerge from the committees to which they are referred, and the majority of these are relatively unimportant measures. Each member of Congress is free to introduce bills, however the most important bills today are those proposed by the executive departments and supported by the President. Although Congress looks to the President to submit his legislative program, it seldom approves his measures without substantial revision.

The quality of debate in the House leaves much to be desired. Many speeches on the floor are designed for home consumption. Few votes are changed by the debates; when in doubt most members rely largely upon the judgment of the committee members of their party rather than upon speeches on the floor.

Debate is virtually a lost art in the House, due in large part to the severe time limitations placed on it. When only a few hours are allowed to debate an important and complex measure, and the allotted time is divided among many members who want to express their views, no member has sufficient time to discuss the various provisions of the bill with any degree of thoroughness. Aware of these limitations, and the fact that debates seldom influence votes, members are not encouraged to prepare for them, and the debates often degenerate into platitudes and clichés, with frequent pleas for support of the President, the party, or the leadership.

In contrast to the practice in the House, the Senate debates major legislative measures at length, and they often merit being called "great debates." Because no limit is played on time that individual senators may speak, until an agreement has been reached to bring the debate to a close and vote, many senators prepare themselves thoroughly and deliver debates that educate and inform their colleagues and the public. The Senate prides itself on being the only major legislative chamber in the world that has no rules restricting the length of time members may speak. Yet time limits are in fact placed on debate, for only by adopting such restrictions can any legislative body transact its business. After a debate on a bill has proceeded for several days and the principal proponents and opponents have made lengthy speeches, the majority leader is usually able to secure a unanimous agreement fixing a time when debate will end and the Senate will vote on the bill and all amendments. By this time everything that can be said for and against the bill has probably been said, and further continuation of the debate would be tedious.

The rule of unlimited debate is often used by a group of senators to prevent the Senate from voting on a measure to which they strongly object, or to delay the vote until they can voice their objections—a practice which is known as the filibuster. The purpose of a filibuster is not to debate the merits of the issue, but rather to prevent a vote from being taken. In 1917 the Senate adopted a cloture rule which can be adopted by a two-thirds vote, but the Senate has seldom voted cloture because of its reluctance to limit debate.

A successful filibuster requires the concerted efforts of senators who are able to prolong debate by lengthy speeches and dilatory tactics until the majority of the Senate agrees to table the measure under consideration, in order to consider essential legislation. Filibustering senators usually make little pretense of speaking on the bill itself; their desks piled high with books and papers, they talk or read on any subject of their choosing.

In recent years the filibuster has been used principally by southern senators to block votes on civil rights legislation, including bills related to the right to vote, segregation, lynching, and fair employment practices. Until the Civil Rights bill of 1964, senators favoring civil rights legislation had tried unsuccessfully to impose cloture. In 1964, cloture (limitation on debate) was invoked successfully and shattered a tradition of long standing.

The filibuster enables a determined minority of senators to prevent legislation which they regard as obnoxious from coming to a vote. Its effect is to require not only a majority of the Senate but a concurrent majority of senators from all major sections of the country to approve proposed legislation. The Constitution protects the rights of minorities as well as of majorities. A group of senators large enough to carry on a successful filibuster and sufficiently determined to withstand the pressure of public opinion can prevent the government from taking an action that their section regards as unacceptable.

The right of members to speak without limit is a highly prized tradition of the Senate and one that it is reluctant to give up. When it is wisely used by senators who are thoroughly prepared and speak on issues of national importance, their lengthy speeches serve to educate the country and to arouse public opinion; however, such speeches are frequently made by senators whose loquacity exceeds their sagacity.

The conduct of investigations has become a major activity of Congress, and one that often receives great public attention. It conducts investigations not only to acquire information to serve as the basis for legislation but also to check on the administration of laws and to inform the public, even though the facts may be well known to the lawmakers. Investigations constitute a powerful weapon of Congress; if used wisely and in the public interest they can be as effective as legislation in correcting shortcomings in the administration of the departments or undesirable practices in the economy or society. Congress often uses investigations to expose conditions or practices that warrant public attention and concern, as, for example, the investigations of organized crime by the Kefauver committee a decade ago.

Since World War II Congress has greatly increased its investigations; they now number about one hundred and cost about $10 million annually. Many of the investigations are politically motivated and are undertaken for publicity rather than reform. Many criticisms have been voiced of congressional investigations in recent years, especially because of the excesses of a few committees. At one time during the height of the McCarthy investigations, Walter Lippmann warned that unless congressional investigations were curbed they would bring about a fundamental change in the Constitution. It cannot be doubted that great harm was done to the security of the country by some of the investigations which professed to safeguard it. Various reforms have been proposed to curb the excesses of a few investigating committees, but Congress is reluctant to change its ways.

Since the end of World War II there has been a continuing demand for the reform and strengthening of Congress. A Congressional Reorganization Act, passed in 1946, resulted in providing Congress with a greatly enlarged staff. Every member of Congress is now provided with several assistants and a clerical staff, and an office both in Washington and in his own district. The standing committees have staffs of considerable size, including experts on the subjects considered by the committee. The expenses of the congressional establishment today exceed $30 million annually, an amount many times greater than that of any other legislative body. Yet the additional staff has not enabled Congress to act wisely and promptly on the great legislative issues presented to it by the President and its own members. The failure of Congress to act on important legislative proposals during the first three years of the Kennedy administration led many thoughtful people to demand further reform of its organization and procedures. The inability of Congress to act on pressing legislation is due largely to its lack of effective, responsible leadership, the dispersion of power among numerous committees, the weak party discipline, traditions such as a rigid rule of

seniority in committee assignments, and the decentralized character of American political parties. Congress
moves slowly in changing its rules and procedures, and
any reforms will be the result of evolutionary rather
than revolutionary changes. In the meantime, the extraordinary political skills of such American presidents as
Lyndon B. Johnson must be exercised in legislative
matters if Congress is to meet the needs of the society.

8 LEGISLATIVE POLICY-MAKING

Hugh Douglas Price

The path by which a bill becomes a law in the United States is a long one. When the proposal is highly controversial, the path can also be very difficult. Opponents of a bill need to be successful only at any one stage of its consideration in order to stop it. But a bill's backers must muster support for it at a series of stages and in different arenas of decision. There is no entirely typical path by which a bill becomes a law, but the major steps in the legislative process are common to most bills.

Somewhere between 15,000 and 20,000 bills are introduced into each Congress. These range in importance from minor bills relating to a local area or the relief of a particular individual to the great issues of national policy. In this essay I shall sketch out the main steps by which the 1963 civil rights recommendations of President Kennedy were modified and debated by Congress, and eventually became the Civil Rights Law of 1964. The hazards which all measures must pass stand out most clearly in the case of a major bill to which there is determined opposition. There is little question that the Civil Rights Bill was the most controversial measure considered by the Eighty-eighth Congress.

ORIGINS OF THE BILL

When the Eighty-eighth Congress convened in January 1963, major action on civil rights legislation did not seem likely. The President had put his major emphasis on a tax reduction measure and other New Frontier legislation and made only minor recommendations in regard to civil rights. Most observers felt that a major push for new civil rights legislation would tie up Congress for so long and split Northern and Southern Democrats so deeply that it would endanger the rest of the Administration's program.

As the spring of 1963 wore on, however, civil rights came more and more to the center of public attention. The limited Civil Rights bills of 1957 and 1960 had sought to guarantee the right of Negroes to register and vote, but in the Deep South they were not proving effective. Negroes in Birmingham and other parts of the South were also resorting to sit-ins, picketing, and boycotts to protest against policies of racial discrimination in hotels, restaurants, lunch counters, and other public accommodations. By May 1963 it was evident that the Kennedy administration would have to decide on some sort of civil rights proposals or face the possibility of more widespread demonstrations and violence. The problem was how to get the demonstrators out of the streets and into the orderly channels of protest through the courts. This was an especially difficult area for the federal government to deal with because it involved subjects dealt with traditionally by the state governments.

The exact source of the various ideas and provisions that go into a major bill is almost impossible to trace.

99

Existing legal provisions and previously proposed bills provide one major source of ideas, and others are added as the work of drafting a proposed measure progresses. The broad outlines of the measure that President Kennedy was to send to Congress were carefully considered by the President, by Attorney General Robert F. Kennedy, and by the staff of the Justice Department (which would be most directly concerned with enforcing the new law, if it were enacted). But many other people also contributed directly or indirectly to the development of the bill.

What President Kennedy finally proposed to Congress, in June 1963, went considerably beyond the area of securing voting rights for Negroes; still, it did not include all the provisions that civil rights leaders were asking for. The four key sections of the proposal were:

1. In regard to voting rights the bill would require the presumption that anyone with a sixth-grade education could meet a state's literacy requirement (thus bypassing the practice of applying unusually stiff and sometimes ambiguous requirements which even Negro Ph.D.'s failed to pass in some localities). It would also authorize the appointment of special voting referees to register Negroes in certain areas.

2. It would require that all businesses providing public accommodations—such as hotels, motels, motion-picture houses, and other public places that substantially affected interstate commerce—be open to all persons regardless of race, color, religion, or national origin.

3. It would authorize technical and financial assistance to schools in the process of desegregating, and permit the Attorney General to file suit for school desegregation if he received a signed complaint.

4. It would declare that government administrators are not required to provide federal grant-in-aid assistance to states or localities found to discriminate.

In addition to these four key provisions the draft bill also provided for the establishment of a Community Relations Service (to help in settling racial disputes), the extension of the life of the Civil Rights Commission for a period of four more years, and gave statutory status to the existing committee on equal employment by firms holding government contracts. By far the greatest amount of public attention, however, was on the proposal to ban discrimination in private businesses providing accommodations for the public.

INTRODUCTION AND REFERRAL TO COMMITTEE

Although bills are often drafted by executive agencies or private groups, they can be introduced officially into the House or Senate only by a member of Congress. Customarily the bills that make up an Administration's program are introduced by the chairman of the committee to which they will be referred (assuming the President's party is in the majority in Congress). If the chairman is opposed to the measure, it may be introduced by another member of the committee or, in the Senate, perhaps by the party floor leader.

In the House of Representatives the Administration's proposed Civil Rights Bill was introduced by Brooklyn Congressman Emanuel Celler, the chairman of the Judiciary Committee (to which it would be routinely assigned) and a strong supporter of civil rights. Other House members could introduce identically worded bills under their own names, thus indicating their support for the proposal. The Judiciary Committee had already received a number of proposed civil rights measures introduced by various Republican members of Congress and by some liberal Democrats. These, however, had little chance of receiving an independent hearing in the committee, which would ordinarily give priority to the Administration's proposals.

In the Senate the situation was a bit more complicated. The chairman of the Senate Judiciary Committee was Senator James Eastland of Mississippi, a leading opponent of civil rights legislation. Also, the Republican minority leader, Senator Everett Dirksen of Illinois, had indicated he was not prepared to support the public accommodations section. As a result, the full Administration bill was introduced by Senator Mansfield, the Democratic majority leader. He and Senator Dirksen then co-sponsored a bill identical to the Administration's proposal except that it omitted the public accommodations section. Finally, a bill dealing only with public accommodations was introduced by Senator Magnuson, the chairman of the Committee on Interstate and Foreign Commerce. Because the federal government's constitutional authority to regulate private businesses rested on the commerce clause of the Constitution, Senator Magnuson's bill would go to his own committee rather than to Senator Eastland's Judiciary Committee.

COMMITTEE HEARINGS

The late start which the Administration had made in civil rights meant that most of the summer was consumed by committee hearings. The greater part of the legislative work of Congress is performed in its committees and subcommittees. On a major bill scores of witnesses are heard: Cabinet officers and others concerned with how it will be carried out, spokesmen of various private interest groups, as well as subject-matter specialists. On the House side of Capitol Hill, hearings were conducted by a Judiciary Committee subcommittee headed by Chairman Celler. The hearings began on June 26, and extended into August. In all, some ninety-one witnesses were heard and a great variety of views were expressed.

Senator Eastland maintained firm control of the Senate Judiciary Committee. He had no intention of reporting out the Administration bill, but he eventually decided to hold some hearings. The hearings consisted largely of a marathon series of appearances by Attorney General Robert F. Kennedy, who was questioned at great length by Senator Ervin of North Carolina. Senator Ervin, a former justice of the North Carolina Supreme Court, criticized the Administration's bill from a variety of legal angles. Like most Southern critics he was unwilling to acknowledge that there was a denial of Negro voting rights in parts of the South or that local practices in regard to discrimination could or should be changed by legislation.

As the long summer wore on, the issue of greatest contention was just how far the federal government should or, under the Constitution, could go in forbidding discrimination in privately owned facilities offering accommodations to the public. By August 1, Attorney General Kennedy was ready to concede that the Administration's bill was not intended to extend to small rooming houses, or to barber shops, beauty shops, or swimming pools (whose involvement in interstate commerce is exceedingly slight). That some such limitation might well be politically necessary was evident from an August survey which indicated no more than fifty-five members of the Senate ready to vote to invoke cloture to break a filibuster against the proposed bill and accommodations provisions. It would, of course, take two-thirds of the senators voting (that is, sixty-seven if all one hundred were present) to put cloture into effect.

The Administration strategy called for action to be taken first in the House of Representatives. There seemed little chance of getting the Senate's Civil Rights Bill out of the Senate Judiciary Committee. Hence the strategy would be to wait until the House bill was passed by the House and sent to the Senate. Parliamentary procedure in the Senate would permit a Civil Rights Bill supporter to object to having the House-passed bill referred to Senator Eastland's committee. A simple majority vote would then be sufficient to have the House-passed bill placed on the Senate calendar. But the question remained: Just what sort of bill would the House pass? The answer was largely in the hands of the House Republican leaders, for they would be the ones to provide the crucial margin of needed House votes.

COMMITTEE "MARK UP" AND AMENDMENTS

After the last witnesses have been heard and controversial questions have exhaustively been pursued, the most crucial work of the committee members begins. This is the detailed "mark up" of the draft bill. Thus attention centered on the activities of Congressman Celler's Judiciary subcommittee. Its members were of several different minds as how to proceed. First, there was the problem of maintaining a bipartisan front such that neither party would receive all the credit for the bill or all the blame for changes made in the bill. This was essential if the Democratic administration was to get the Republican support it needed to make up for the almost solid opposition of Southern Democrats. Second, some of the pro-civil rights liberals on the subcommittee felt that the bill should be expanded to include a variety of additional provisions on the theory that concessions would have to be made at later stages of the legislative process.

Administration strategists were more concerned with getting a firm bipartisan agreement on a draft and sticking to it than with the idea of expanding the bill and risking a process of opening it up to a variety of amendments. They feared that, once begun, the whittling process would get out of hand and then it would be difficult to uphold a united Republican–Northern Democratic front.

Within the House Judiciary subcommittee things became both bitter and confusing. The group that favored strengthening the Administration's bill was arguing for proposals which the Republicans were unwilling to go along with. Many Negro civil rights leaders also favored strengthening the bill. Finally, they swung Chairman Celler to a position in favor of a much more sweeping proposal than that originally suggested by the Administration. The draft that the subcommittee majority decided to report out to the full House Judiciary Committee extended the public accommodations section to cover all facilities licensed by a state or locality (rather than those with a substantial connection to interstate commerce), established a Fair Employment Practices Commission with its own enforcement powers, and required the mandatory cutoff of federal grants and aid to projects found to discriminate (rather than just authorizing such cutoff).

The subcommittee's action was greeted with enthusiasm by most Negro civil rights spokesmen, but it left the Administration in a difficult position. As it stood, the subcommittee bill was not acceptable to enough Republicans to be approved by the full Judiciary Committee, or by the Rules Committee, or by a vote of the House. It would certainly not prove acceptable to the Senate, where a two-thirds majority would probably be needed to break the expected Southern filibuster. Yet, if the subcommittee draft were to be cut back in some respects ("watered down," as the proponents of the more sweeping measure put it), then the Administration itself would have to take the political responsibility for doing so. The Republicans in the House could not afford to have the Democrats get credit for being willing to go all the way and then having to cut the bill back. The blame for cutting back the subcommittee version would have to be shouldered by the Administration.

In this delicate situation Attorney General Kennedy testified on October 15 and 16 before the full committee. He argued bluntly for cutting back the subcommittee draft into a more realistic program on which Republicans and Northern Democrats could unite. "What I want is a bill, not an issue," he said. This brought some angry criticism from Negro civil rights leaders, and it appeared that the supporters of the Administration constituted only a minority of the Judiciary Committee. They would clearly need the support of most of the committee's Republican members. There was even talk that some of the Southern Democrats on the committee, who opposed any bill, would join with the more extreme civil rights supporters to back the subcommittee draft (which the Southerners felt could be defeated or side-tracked).

Meetings of the full committee scheduled for October 23 and 24 were canceled while the Administration sought to retrieve the situation. On the 23rd, President Kennedy met with Judiciary Committee Chairman Emanuel Celler and Republican Congressman McCulloch, the ranking minority member of the committee, plus House Speaker John W. McCormack and Republican Minority Leader Charles Halleck. After several days of intensive efforts a compromise was reached between the Administration and the Republican leadership. Final agreement on the new bipartisan draft was reached at an informal meeting on October 28. It was sprung on the full Judiciary Committee, without further hearings, on the following day. In quick order the committee voted down a motion to report out the far-reaching subcommittee bill, 15 to 19 (with several Southerners joining the more ardent civil rights advocates to vote for it). A motion to substitute the new bipartisan draft was then carried, 20 to 14. On this the Democrats were split 12 to 8 in favor of the motion; Republicans were split 8 to 6 in favor. Finally, the committee voted to report out to the House the bipartisan compromise bill.

The bipartisan compromise went substantially beyond the Kennedy administration's original draft, but it retreated in several particulars from the more ambitious subcommittee draft. The new compromise retained the mandatory cutoff of federal aid to programs which did not take steps to eliminate discrimination. But the enforcement powers in regard to Fair Employment Practices (now referred to as Equal Employment Opportunity) were left to the courts, and the Attorney General was authorized to *intervene* in private suits contesting segregation but not to *initiate* such suits. President Kennedy and the Attorney General commended the Republican House leaders for having put "political differences . . . aside in the interest of meeting an urgent national crisis."

Within the Judiciary Committee the advocates of the all-out subcommittee draft had, in a way, pursued their strategy of asking for everything and then allowing some of the additions to be eliminated. At the conclusion of committee consideration they could point to a bill that indeed went considerably beyond what the Administration had originally asked. Subsequently, however, the strategy was to be dominated by the need for maintaining a bipartisan front in the face of all other major proposed changes in the course of House consideration. In the Senate some further revision seemed likely, but that was to be carried out on the basis of bipartisan negotiations between the Administration and Republican leaders rather than by opening the bill up to wholesale floor amendment.

THE RULES COMMITTEE AND THE HOUSE CALENDAR

When bills are reported out of committee in final form and an accompanying committee report explains their provisions, they are put on one of the House calendars. In the nineteenth century the regular order of House business was to move down the items on a calendar, taking them up in order, but eventually there were hundreds of bills and the most important or most urgent were often far down on the various bill calendars. To speed action the House Committee on Rules adopted the practice of granting a special resolution providing that a given bill, regardless of its place on the calendar, be taken up and considered.

Before long it became the practice for almost all major legislation, except appropriation bills, to come to the floor by means of a special resolution. The Rules Committee became a sort of super-policy committee and a potential legislative bottleneck. If a majority of its members refused to vote for a special resolution, or "rule" as it is commonly called, to bring up a major bill, then the bill would probably be stalled. The extraordinary procedures for bypassing the Rules Committee are complicated and awkward to use.

After a bitter floor battle in 1963 the membership of the Rules Committee had been expanded from twelve (eight Democrats and four Republicans) to fifteen (ten Democrats and five Republicans). On most measures other than civil rights the Administration could count on eight loyal Democratic supporters, although the two senior Democratic members, both from the South, would often vote with the committee's five Republicans. On civil rights, however, none of the Southern Democrats on the Rules Committee were likely to vote for a resolution to bring the bill to the floor. The Northern Democrats would need the support of at least some of the Republican members of the Rules Committee. Here again the necessity for a bipartisan front was clear. The Republican leadership had indicated that Republican members of the Rules Committee would, in due course, vote with the Northern Democrats to report the bill to the House floor.

The bipartisan Civil Rights Bill was finally reported out of the Judiciary Committee, accompanied by a written report with dissents by the bill's opponents, on November 20. Congressman Howard W. Smith, chairman of the Rules Committee, was known to oppose the bill and expected to delay as long as possible in granting a rule for its floor consideration. Then, just two days later, President Kennedy was assassinated in Dallas. As the shocked nation began to return to normal after the tragic event it became increasingly clear that the Civil Rights Bill probably could not be pushed through the House in the time remaining before Christmas adjournment. Congressman Smith continued to delay scheduling hearings on granting a rule, and Republicans were unwilling to support a move to resort to a discharge petition.

On December 5, Congressman Smith relented and announced that he would schedule hearings on granting a rule for the Civil Rights Bill "reasonably soon in January." Such hearings are usually brief, with perhaps forty minutes devoted to comments from the chairman and the ranking minority member of the committee reporting a bill. On civil rights, however, many individual congressmen from the South requested permission to testify, so that the hearings stretched out to the end of January. Finally, on January 30, the members of the Rules Committee voted 11 to 4 to grant a rule to permit consideration of H.R. 7152, the Civil Rights Bill.

HOUSE FLOOR ACTION

Of the major hurdles that the bill faced on the House side, actual floor debate was among the less important. The most difficult had been the development of a bipartisan consensus within the Judiciary Committee. The floor debate continued from February 1 to February 10, but the Southern opponents of the bill found themselves both outnumbered and outorganized. The members of the Democratic Study Group, an informal group of liberal Democrats, organized a "buddy system" so that each of twenty key members helped to keep track of the whereabouts of five or six other members. Taking no chances, the pro-civil rights lobbying groups had "watchers" stationed in the House galleries who would contact a friendly congressman if they noted that one of the members they were to check on was not in attendance. This ensured that a pro-civil rights majority would always be on hand, even for voice votes.

The Southerners concentrated their criticism on the

public accommodations, fair employment, and cutoff of federal funds provisions and the need to guarantee a local jury trial in cases arising from court orders issued in civil rights cases. On amendments they were seldom able to muster more than about 100 votes. Except for a few minor amendments the bipartisan bill remained intact. The final House vote for passage was by a margin of 290 to 130. Northern and Western Democrats were for passage by a margin of 141 to 4; Southern Democrats were against passage 92 to 11. Of the 177 Republicans voting, 138 voted for the bill and 34 against. Thus it was a bipartisan victory for the bipartisan bill. Its next, and more severe, test would come in the Senate.

SENATE FILIBUSTER

In the Senate the Civil Rights Bill would face the unique difficulty of a Southern filibuster. Ordinarily any senator can speak for as long as he likes on a bill or amendment, so a determined group of senators with a long series of amendments can talk a bill to death. On most routine bills the Senate, by unanimous consent, will voluntarily set a time for ending debate. In the case of a full-scale filibuster the only practical way to force a vote is by imposing cloture. Under Rule XXII of the Senate Rules cloture limits each senator to one hour of further debate, but cloture can be imposed only by a vote of two-thirds of the senators voting.

When the House-passed bill reached the Senate there was little doubt but that a simple majority of senators could be found who favored it with little or no change. But the eighteen Southern Democratic senators, aided by one Southern Republican senator, could hold the floor in relays and thereby prevent the bill from coming to a vote. Attempts to impose cloture in eleven previous civil rights debates had been uniformly unsuccessful, although cloture had been imposed on a few occasions involving other matters. Many senators from states with small populations, such as the states of the Rocky Mountain area and the Southwest, traditionally are reluctant to vote to impose cloture against any filibuster. These senators represent states with few votes in the House of Representatives, and hence their equal weight in the Senate, enforced if necessary by the filibuster, is regarded as highly important.

By a rarely used parliamentary procedure the Civil Rights Bill, now fifty-five pages in length, was put on the Senate calendar of bills rather than referred to the Senate Judiciary Committee. This served to bypass Senator Eastland of Mississippi, the chairman of that committee. But the bill still faced the danger of the Southern filibuster, or rather of two possible filibusters. To bring the bill to the floor of the Senate would require a motion which itself would be debatable, and at filibuster length if the Southerners so desired. Even after that motion was accepted there would still be unlimited debate on the actual passage of the bill. This debate was expected to continue until some compromise was reached, which seemed unlikely, or until a two-thirds majority was convinced of the need to impose cloture. This would not be easy.

The Senate debate on the preliminary motion to take up the bill began on March 9 and continued for sixteen days. After this preliminary test of their lung power, the Southern bloc relented and permitted a vote on the question of considering the bill. This was passed by a 67 to 17 margin, and made H.R. 7152 the pending business before the Senate. At this point the pro-civil rights senators took the center of the stage for almost two weeks with a series of major floor speeches outlining the intent, effect, and need for the various provisions of the bill.

The key to the outcome in the Senate obviously rested with the position of the Senate Republicans. Only they could provide the necessary margin of votes to impose cloture and thus bring the Southern filibuster to an end. Senator Dirksen of Illinois, the Republican minority leader, had been unhappy over the inclusion of a federal fair employment practices provision in the bill and had also expressed doubts about the public accommodations section. As the Southern filibuster ground on, Senator Dirksen met with other Republican senators to seek some consensus on proposed amendments to the bill which, if acceptable to the Administration, might bring more Republicans into the ranks of those ready to vote for cloture. Clearly there would have to be some modification of the House bill, but if the changes went too far there was a possibility that House Republicans would not agree to the Senate bill. A conference committee to adjust differences between the two houses would be awkward, because its action would have to be approved by the Senate, and thus risk another filibuster.

Early in May the Southern bloc, headed by Senator Richard Russell of Georgia, indicated that they were willing to bring the proposed amendment relating to jury trials to a vote, but they would continue their filibuster against the bill. In a series of votes on amendments the pro-civil rights senators were able to defeat the more sweeping proposals for a jury trial in all cases arising under the act, which they felt would undermine enforcement of the bill in many Deep South areas.

If all one hundred senators were present it would take sixty-seven senators to impose cloture and thus end the filibuster. By mid-May it appeared that Majority Leader Mansfield and Minority Leader Dirksen could count on about sixty firm cloture supporters, with twenty-nine senators firmly opposed to cloture. The balance rested with the remaining eleven senators, who were still uncommitted. Several had indicated particular provisions of the bill that they objected to or indicated that the time had not yet come to cut off the debate.

Senator Dirksen met in a series of sessions with Senator Hubert Humphrey, the bill's floor manager, and Attorney General Kennedy in an attempt to work out a number of amendments that would be acceptable to the Administration but also serve to win over additional cloture votes. Meanwhile, in order to build up public support for the bill in Western states with very few Negro residents, civil rights supporters turned to religious and church groups. These groups had become increasingly committed to the civil rights cause as a moral issue; therefore, they could provide some grass-roots enthusiasm for the bill even in distant rural states.

As the filibuster moved into its eleventh week of continuous debate, Senator Dirksen was ready to present his revised version of the bill. The revision he had worked out with the Administration now ran to seventy-four pages. In general it followed the pattern of the House bill, but it reduced the discretion of the attorney general, spelled out a number of things not to be effected by the bill, and gave states with their own public accommodations laws an opportunity to settle disputes before the federal government intervened. The long-awaited vote on applying cloture was expected on Tuesday, June 9. Several conservative Republican senators, however, were still not entirely satisfied with Senator Dirksen's revised bill and requested that the leadership permit votes on some of their proposed amendments prior to imposing cloture. This was agreeable both to Senator Russell, leader of the Southern bloc, and to the civil rights leaders, who postponed the cloture vote to June 10.

When time came for the cloture vote the Senate's public galleries were packed with spectators, many of whom were Negroes. Senator Russell summarized his opposition to the pending measure, while the case for cloture and passage of the bill was presented by Senators Humphrey, Mansfield, and Dirksen. Perhaps the most dramatic appeal came from Senator Dirksen when he quoted Victor Hugo's statement: "Stronger than all the armies is an idea whose time has come." He continued as follows: "The time has come for equality of opportunity in sharing in government, in education, and in employment. It will not be stayed or denied. It is here."

The clerk began to call the roll, beginning with Senator Aiken of Vermont, and then on down the list in alphabetical order. All one hundred senators were present, including one senator who had been brought from his hospital bed. It would take 67 votes to apply cloture, and the sixty-seventh vote came from Senator Williams of Delaware. The final total was 71 senators for cloture and 29 opposed. The majority included 44 Democratic senators and 27 Republicans; the minority consisted of 23 Democrats, mostly from the South, and 6 Republicans, including Senator Goldwater.

SENATE PASSAGE OF THE BILL

With the cloture time limit in effect a vote on the bill itself could not be long delayed. Southern senators had filed over five hundred amendments, but they would have only one hour apiece to call them up; no major amendments were in fact accepted. The vote on passage of the much modified bill came on June 19, 1964, exactly one year after President Kennedy's request to Congress for legislation in the civil rights field. This was the eighty-third day of the Senate debate on the measure. Since only a simple majority was needed for passage there was no doubt of the outcome. The bill was passed 73 to 27.

Because the Senate-passed bill was different from the bill approved by the House, there was still the necessity of winning House approval of the Senate version. Then the measure would go to the White House for President Johnson's approval, after which it would be part of the law of the land.

HOUSE APPROVAL OF SENATE BILL

The House was expected to accept the Senate version of the bill and thus avoid the need for a conference committee and subsequent action by both chambers. But to bring the Senate bill to the House floor would require either unanimous consent, which the Southerners would block, or a special rule from the Rules Committee. There was a week's delay in forcing a meeting of the Rules Committee, over the objections of its chairman, Congressman Smith of Virginia. On June 30, however, the committee met and voted the resolution to bring the Senate version to the House floor with only one hour provided for debate.

The bill was easily passed by the House, with 153 Democrats and 136 Republicans voting aye. There had been suggestions that President Johnson might wait to sign the bill officially on July 4th, but he decided to give his approval immediately. The chief congressional and senatorial figures involved in the bill's passage were invited to the White House, together with Cabinet members and executive branch leaders, for the final ceremony. The signing took place in the East Room of the

White House at 6:45 P.M. on July 2, 1964. The ceremony was seen on nationwide television, and President Johnson followed the traditional practice of using a series of pens while signing the bill, then giving the pens to the key backers of the bill.

The civil rights proposals were now law. Even though the provisions did not include everything that some civil rights supporters wanted, they did mark a major step forward. The debate on the bill, and especially over Senate cloture, had been long and thorough, but it had not degenerated into bitterness. The legislative process had done its work, and in the process it had helped to mold a bill more acceptable to most Americans and yet strong enough to protect and expand the civil rights of all Americans who might face local discrimination.

9 THE AMERICAN PARTY SYSTEM

E. E. Schattschneider

No one now living in the United States can remember when the contest began between the Democratic and the Republican parties. It has been going on for more than a century, making it one of the oldest political rivalries in the world.

The American political system is a classical example of the two-party system. When we say that we have a two-party system in the United States we do not mean that we have only two parties. Usually about a dozen parties nominate presidential candidates. We call it a two-party system because we have two large parties and a number of small parties, and the large parties are so large that we often forget about the rest. Usually the small parties collectively poll less than 5 per cent of the vote cast in national elections.

The Democratic and Republican parties are the largest and most competitive organizations in the American community. They organize the electorate very simply by maintaining the two-party system. Americans almost inevitably become Democrats or Republicans because there is usually no other place for them to go. Moreover, because the rivalry of these parties is very old, most Americans know where they belong in the system.

118

As a consequence of the dominance of the major parties, most elected officials are either Republicans or Democrats, including all Presidents and nearly all senators and national representatives, all state governors, and nearly all local officials. Attempts to break up this old system have been made in every presidential election in the past one hundred years, but the system has survived all assaults.

How does it happen that the two-party system is so strongly rooted in American politics? The explanation is probably to be found in the way elections are conducted. In the United States, unlike countries with a parliamentary system of government, we elect not only the President, but a host of other executives, about 800,000 of them. We also elect congressmen from single-member districts. For example, we elect 435 members of the House of Representatives from 435 districts (there are a few exceptions), one member for each district. Statistically, this kind of election favors the major parties. The system of elections makes it easy for the major parties to maintain their dominant position, because they are apt to win more than their share of the offices.

Great consequences result from the stability of the two-party system. Whereas minor parties are likely to identify themselves with special interests or special programs and thus take extreme positions, the major parties are so large that they tend to be moderate. Goldwater Republicanism challenged this tendency and met overwhelming defeat in 1964. No extremist has ever been elected President of the United States. If moderation is a virtue in politics, the two-party system has much to recommend it.

Another consequence of the system is that it produces majorities automatically. Because there are only two competitors in the running, it is almost inevitable that one will receive a majority. Moreover, the system tends slightly to exaggerate the victory of the winning party. This is not always true, but the strong tendency to produce majorities is built into the system.

In 175 years of constitutional history, Americans have learned much about the way in which the system can be managed so as to make possible the peaceful transfer of power from one party to the other. At the level of presidential elections, the party in power has been overturned by the party out of power fifteen times, almost once a decade. In the election of 1860, the political system broke down, and the Civil War, the worst disaster in American history, resulted. Our history justifies our confidence in the system but also shows that it is not foolproof.

The second major party is able to survive a defeat because the statistical tendency that exaggerates the victory of the winning party operates even more strongly in favor of the second party against the third, fourth, and fifth parties. As a result, the defeated major party is able to maintain a monopoly of the opposition. The advantage of the second party over the third is so great that it is the only party that is likely to be able to overturn the party in power. It is able, therefore, to attract the support of everyone seriously opposed to the party in power. The second party is important as long as it can monopolize the movement to overthrow the party in power, because it is certain to come into power sooner or later. Evidence of the strength of the opposition is seen in that the losing party has won less than one-third of the seats in the national House only twice in the fifteen most recent elections and has polled less than 40 per cent of the vote in only one presidential election in the past generation.

Evidence of the moderation of the major parties is that much business is conducted across party lines. What happens when the Democrats control one house of Congress and the Republicans control the other? About the same volume of legislation is passed as when one party controls both houses, although some important legislation is likely to be blocked temporarily. It is possible to carry on the work of the government even when party control is divided because party differences are not fundamental.

People unfamiliar with American politics are often puzzled by the great emphasis Americans place on the nomination of party candidates for public office. Why such a fuss over the way the parties choose their candidates? The American form of government has something to do with the way the parties act. The task of selecting party leaders in the responsible cabinet system of government is performed by the parliamentary party. In the United States, the President is not a member of Congress and presidential and congressional elections are legally separate.

The selection of presidential candidates is complicated by the fact that Presidents are limited to two terms, and unsuccessful candidates are not usually nominated a second time. Thus the opposition party nearly always has an open contest for the nomination and the party in power frequently is in this position too. In 1964 there was no contest in the Democratic party because President Johnson was eligible for election and was unopposed in this bid for the Democratic nomination. On the other hand, there was more than one candidate for the Republican nomination, even if majority sentiment in the Republican national convention was clearly for Goldwater.

121

Parties have usually been able to iron out the difficulties created when a few persons have wanted nominations; sometimes, however, they have failed to produce an agreement on a single candidate. Whenever parties have failed to unite behind one nominee, the result has been disastrous. In 1836, when there were three Whig candidates for the Presidency, Martin Van Buren, the Democratic nominee, won the election. In 1860 two Democratic candidates were nominated by rival Democratic conventions, and Abraham Lincoln, the Republican candidate, was elected with about 40 per cent of the vote. At the 1912 Republican national convention, the delegates supporting Theodore Roosevelt for the nomination walked out when Mr. Taft was nominated and then held a convention of their own in which they nominated Mr. Roosevelt. With two Republican candidates in the contest, Woodrow Wilson, the Democratic candidate, won easily.

American nominating procedures have been based on the assumption that there are likely to be a great many contests for nominations. Therefore, Americans have developed formal and public procedures for settling these contests. For a period of several months every election year we are likely to hear more about contests *within* the parties than about contests *between* the parties. Later, when the nominations have been made, the election campaign, the contest between the parties, begins. An American election is a two-stage affair. At the end of the first stage the parties close ranks behind their nominees; in the second stage they compete for votes in the election itself.

A look at the history of American parties will show how present-day nominating procedures have developed. In the early days of the Republic, presidential nominations were made by a congressional caucus, by the congressional party. This is how Madison and Monroe were nominated 150 years ago. This system ran into trouble in 1824 because the opposition party, the Federalist Party, collapsed and went out of business. Thereafter, a nomination by the congressional caucus of the Jeffersonian party amounted to something much like an appointment to the Presidency. The attack on the caucus, especially by Andrew Jackson, destroyed it. It was only after a number of years that national conventions were used to make presidential nominations. By 1840 both parties began to use national conventions to select their presidential nominees and the national conventions, consisting of delegates from all of the states, still look very much the way they did 145 years ago.

No matter how nominations are made, one point to be kept in mind is that American parties decide nearly everything when they make nominations. Because the issue in elections is usually a broad question of confidence in the party in power, the party nomination is a bid for confidence—confidence in the ability and determination of the candidate and the party to meet the problems that lie ahead. When a party chooses a presidential candidate it says to the country, in effect, "Trust us under the leadership of this man to cope with the visible and the unknown problems that are going to come up for decision in the next four years."

No party could ever spell out in detail everything that it is going to do when it comes into power. A party platform is not a contract between the party and the public but a declaration of its attitudes and tendencies. Sometimes this declaration is specific, but more often it is general—and the public probably does not want very much more. Problems of public policy are too complex and too unpredictable for political commitments that bind parties hand and foot to a program which gives them no latitude to cope with new situations and no opportunity to work out new solutions. The parties deal with this by adopting statements of general party policies and by nominating candidates at the same time.

How are the American people divided in their allegiance to the two parties? A generation ago the party division was along geographical lines. The Republican party drew its support chiefly from the northern and western areas of the country and the Democratic party was largely a southern party. This political regionalism has a special name in American politics—Americans call it sectionalism. Before 1932 the party alignment was so sharply sectional that the Republican party almost ceased to exist in the southern states and the Democratic party was very weak in the northern and western states. One result was that although a two-party system existed in the country as a whole, there were many states in which one party became so dominant that the people had very little choice. Since 1932 this system has been breaking up and is now being displaced by a national party division.

Between 1924 and 1952 the Republican vote in the old Democratic South increased sixfold while the Democratic vote in the old Republican strongholds in the North increased fivefold. The new tendency was illustrated in the 1960 election in which Mr. Kennedy polled less than 40 per cent of the vote in only three of the fifty states and more than 60 per cent in only two states.

The displacement of the old regional party alignment by the new national alignment is likely to have important consequences. One consequence is a great increase in the competitiveness of the parties or, perhaps more accurately, an increase in the area of competition. A generation ago party competition was largely restricted to a few states in which the parties contested elections on a relatively equal basis. Now there has been a great increase in the number of two-party states, states in which the parties compete on even terms. This change is likely to alter power relations in the national government.

By far the most interesting of the historic political regions in the United States is the old Solid South, thus named because of its solid support of the Democratic party for many decades. The Solid South consists of the eleven states which joined the Southern Confederacy during the Civil War, 1861–1865. The hostility of the South to the Republican party dates back to the war.

The historic attachment of the South to the Democratic party was upset by the election of 1932, one of the most important elections in American history. In this election the Democratic vote in the northern and western regions of the country increased so sensationally that the party outgrew its old southern base and became substantially a new party. The Democratic vote in twelve important northern states increased from 2.5 million to 13.5 million. In other words, it became a national party. In four successive elections Mr. Roosevelt won by national majorities so large that he became independent of the South. Since that time relations between the northern and southern wings of the Democratic party have often been bad. On the other hand, the Republican vote in the South has grown rapidly, from 700,000 in 1924 to 4.8 million in 1960.

These voting trends show that a new national party alignment is displacing the old regional pattern. Voting trends seem to show that the Solid South, the last remaining of the old sections of the old regional party alignment, is breaking up. Republican gains in the

125

South are so great that the Republican party in 1962 made a serious effort to win congressional seats in that area, and in 1964 Senator Goldwater's *only* victories came in Arizona and in five states of the Solid South. There is every reason to believe that this regional Republican victory is but a temporary aberration from the general tendency of the two major parties to reflect national interests and forces.

In the American governmental system the President is expected to submit his legislative program to Congress, but Congress is free to revise it or reject it and the President has no way to force the issue except by waiting for public opinion to persuade Congress to move. This is true even when the President's party has a majority in both houses of Congress. The President cannot dissolve Congress and call for a new election to resolve his conflicts with Congress. When the breach in the Democratic party developed in the 1930s, conservative southern congressmen opposed to some of the policies of the national Democratic leadership felt free to vote with the Republican opposition to block parts of the President's legislative program. As a result of this coalition of Republicans and Southern Democrats there have been times when neither party had effective control of Congress.

The difficulties I have described resulted in much criticism of the party system, of Congress, and even of the constitutional system itself. We are now in a position to see that the root of the problem was not in the governmental structure or in the organization of Congress, or in the party system, but in the slow shift from the old sectional political alignment to the new national alignment. The Solid South was, in a way, a classical instance of the old sectional form of political organization. It has taken almost a generation to substitute a new system for the old one. Now we can see a new political order emerging.

What is the difference between the Democratic and Republican parties today? Both are moderate. Both are loyal to the democratic system and both support the free enterprise system. It is reasonable to suppose, however, that in a democratic and capitalistic system tension between government and business will arise. In fact, this tension is built into the political system. The Democratic party has tended, therefore, to become the government party and the Republican party has tended to become the party of business. To say this is to oversimplify the truth; we are speaking only of tendencies, of political differences, of relative differences. Nevertheless, the over-all tendencies of both parties are well established and well understood, provided we do not push the proposition to an extreme.

In the American community everybody wants freedom and a high standard of living, and a party conflict meets the needs of most Americans very well.

The rise of modern industry and the modern business corporation has created a powerful business community. The function of American politics is to reconcile the conflicting needs of democracy and the economy. The American way of dealing with big business has been to develop a big democracy, big enough and powerful enough to offset it. Big business is unavoidably powerful. Americans love their government because it is strong enough and democratic enough to match business power, to police the business system, to supplement business, and to keep business from destroying our liberties.

Americans do not like any of the usual resolutions of the conflict of government and business. They reject the fascist resolution in which business takes over the government; they reject the communist solution in which the government takes over business because they believe that the concentration of all economic and political power in the same hands inevitably becomes oppressive.

We think that the public interest resides in the no man's land between government and business. The public wants to preserve its options, which it would lose if either the fascist or the communist resolutions were adopted. The public likes competitive power systems. It wants both democracy and a high standard of living and thinks it can have both if it can maintain a dynamic equilibrium between the democratic and the capitalist elements in the regime. The public is willing to try to get along with the capitalist system if it can maintain alongside of it a democratic political system powerful enough to police it.

The American party system embodies the American idea of the creative relation of government and business. This is why the Republican party is able to act as the guardian of the free enterprise system without becoming disloyal to the democratic system. This is why the Democratic party is able to espouse the governmental side of the controversy without ever having sought or received a mandate to abolish the capitalist system.

Detailed statements of party principles and policies are not important when the party differences are built into the very structure of the political system.

Because the two major parties are competitive, the public can hold the party in power responsible for its conduct of the government. It can turn the party in power out, as it has done about once a decade throughout American history. In a presidential election the American voter does not base his decision on a detailed party program. The system is so old and the political tendencies of the parties so well known that most American voters know where they belong. As nearly as possible, a national election is a vote of confidence or lack of confidence in the party in power. As long as the elections remain important, the parties will be important also because they are the only organizations that can win elections.

10 ELECTIONS

Donald Herzberg

A century ago, John Bright, an Englishman and a close friend of Abraham Lincoln, had this to say about American presidential elections:

> We know what an election is in the United States for President of the Republic. Every four years there springs from the vote created by the whole people a President over that great nation. I think the whole world offers no finer spectacle than this; it offers no higher dignity; there is no greater object of ambition on the political state on which men are permitted to move. You may point, if you will, to hereditary rulers, to crowns coming down through successive generations of the same family, to thrones based on prescription or on conquest, to scepters wielded over veteran legions in subject realms. But to my mind there is nothing more worthy of reverence and obedience and nothing more sacred than the authority of the freely chosen magistrate of a great and free people; and if there be on earth and amongst men any right divine to govern, surely it rests with the ruler so chosen and so appointed.

Since that eloquent statement was made, the very face and every facet of life in the United States have undergone great change. The expansion of the nation to fifty states, the population explosion, two world wars, a civil war, and a massive industrial revolution have all served to focus great attention on the United States.

In 1860 the population of the United States was about 32 million people; today it is more than 190 million. In 1860 fewer than 5 million votes were cast when Abraham Lincoln was elected President; in 1964, almost 68 million Americans voted, a million or so under the record vote of 69 million cast in 1960. As the people of the United States approach the forty-fifth time that a President is being chosen, the basic question remains: How does a free society such as the United States organize itself so that, despite complexity and great diversity, it may choose its leaders and survive?

At the heart of our government is the electoral system. While the base of suffrage in the United States has gradually been broadened to include more and more citizens, a free and unfettered suffrage has always been a basic cornerstone of our system. Government in the United States rests upon consent of the governed and that consent is gained through the ballot box. It is important to remember that our electoral system calls for regularly scheduled elections. We can predict with absolute certainty when we shall elect our Presidents, members of Congress, our governors, mayors, school board members, coroners, and so forth. Since our creation as a nation we have never failed to hold an election —national, state, or local—on schedule. This record of electoral stability is unparalleled.

Yet our record of citizen participation in these elections is not so satisfactory. Another cause for concern is that our record of citizen participation has grown less as the base of that participation has broadened. Our rate of participation was higher in the last quarter of the nineteenth century than it ever has been in the twentieth century.

It is especially interesting to contrast our voting record with the voting records of other nations of the free world. Many of these nations consistently have a higher rate of participation than we do. It is important to point out that in a strict sense voting turnout figures from other nations are not directly comparable with turnout figures in the United States. Foreign participation statistics normally reflect the percentage of *eligible* voters who voted. The number of eligibles in foreign statistics normally does *not* include aliens and persons who fail to satisfy literacy or residence requirements. United States election figures, on the other hand, reflect the percentage of voters among the *total* population of voting age. Thus the different bases of calculation tend to inflate foreign participation figures and deflate United States figures.

Nevertheless, citizens of other nations vote in greater relative numbers than do Americans. More than 92 per cent of eligible Italian citizens have voted in each of their last four national elections. West Germany has turned out from 78.5 to 87.8 per cent for federal elections during the past fifteen years. Canada maintains its participation percentage at 80 per cent or better. All of the Scandinavian countries consistently turn out well over 80 per cent of their voters.

Although there undoubtedly are many explanations for the better turnout record in other nations, it is significant that the United States has the only system of voting in which the burden of becoming registered and thus eligible to vote falls upon the individual. In other countries the government assumes that responsibility. In Canada, for example, enumerators paid by the government must visit every dwelling in their jurisdiction and register each eligible person. The United States is also the only federal system of government in which the national government does not handle the election and registration details for the election of national officers. In the United States, each of the fifty states devises its own laws and procedures for the conduct of all elections held within the state.

The reasons for our relatively low turnout figures fall into two main categories, psychological and institutional. Psychological factors play an important role. Many political studies have been conducted in an attempt to ascertain who are likely to be nonvoters. Most studies conclude that the most important factor in determining whether a person will vote is his identification with one of our two major political parties. If he feels himself to be either a Democrat or a Republican, he is more likely to vote than if he feels no such kinship. The stronger the identification, the stronger the motivation to register and vote. Participation is likely to be greater if the person who identifies with a party can be made to feel that the election is close and that every vote is needed.

Studies also demonstrate that levels of education and economic status affect voting participation. The more formal an educational experience a citizen has had, the more likely he is to register and vote. As financial status and stability rises, again the likelihood of electoral participation also rises.

In addition to education and economic status, characteristics of sex and age are reflected in participation figures. Voter participation among women in the United States is approximately 10 per cent lower than among men. Voting studies consistently reveal that women are less likely to be motivated by politics and campaigns than are men. Since there are about 4 million more women than men in the United States, the failure of so many women to vote is statistically significant.

Age, too, has an influence upon voter participation. The younger voters tend to vote the least. The age group between twenty-one (the legal voting age in forty-six of our states) and thirty-four has the poorest turnout; the age group between thirty-five and fifty-four has the highest; after age fifty-four voting tends to decline slowly.

The greatest factors in keeping the vote down are institutional—the rules, regulations, and practices within each of the states. If everyone who had wished to vote in 1960 had voted, it is estimated that an additional 24 million votes would have been cast. This would have brought the voter participation figure up from 63.8 to a respectable 81 per cent.

Let us turn our attention to this problem of institutional barriers to voting.

Constitutional responsibilities for elections are divided between the national government and the government in each of the fifty states. To some degree every election held in the United States is within the jurisdiction of both the national government and the states. For instance, even elections for state or local officials, governors and mayors, are held under both federal and state law, for the national government has the power under the Fourteenth, Fifteenth, and Nineteenth Amendments to the Constitution to intervene to prevent discrimination because of race or sex.

In 1964 the people of the United States ratified an amendment to the Constitution which made it unlawful for any state to levy a poll tax on any voter who wants to cast his vote for President and Vice-President and for members of Congress. It is hoped that the five states which presently levy such a tax will now end this practice for all elections as well as those for President and Congress.

The basic philosophic question is, however, how and where to draw the line between the power of the federal government and the individual states. Where should this line be drawn in regard to the election of a President and a Vice-President and the election of congressmen and senators? Traditionally and historically, the states have played the major role in the formulation of election law. The Constitution, however, is quite specific in stating that "the times, places and manner of holding elections for Senators and Representatives shall be prescribed in each state by the legislature thereof, but the Congress may at any time by law make or alter such regulations. . . ."

Congress has been extremely careful, except in the area of laws dealing with corrupt practices and campaign expenditures, to leave the matter up to the states. In fact, in the 1870s, when Congress enacted the law that made the first Tuesday after the first Monday in November the general election day, they were careful to exclude from this law any state whose constitution might be in conflict. Thus it was not until 1958 that Maine got around to altering its state constitution to change the election date for Maine senators and congressmen from September to November.

The Constitution treats elections for President of the United States differently because, technically speaking, the President and the Vice-President are elected only indirectly by the vote of the people; they are chosen by a constitutional body called the Electoral College. This electoral body was devised by the founding fathers in an effort to keep the heat and passions of an election campaign away from the selection of the President. Each state, the Constitution directs, "shall appoint in such manner as the legislature thereof may direct a number of electors equal to the whole number of Senators and Representatives to which the state may be entitled in Congress." The body of these electors from all fifty states is known as the Electoral College. These electors meet in their own states in mid-December and cast their votes for President.

The founding fathers, however, did not foresee the rapid development of our two-party system which quickly altered and diminished the power of the Electoral College. In actual practice today in the states, electors are chosen by each of the two major parties. These electors in almost all states are pledged to support the candidates for President and Vice-President nominated by their party at the national convention. A voter in 1960 technically was not voting directly for either Senator Kennedy or Vice-President Nixon but was instead voting for a group of men and women equal in number to the size of the state's congressional delegation who were pledged to vote for the major candidates. If more people in a state voted for the group of electors pledged to Vice-President Nixon's election, he won the state and was credited with that state's total electoral vote. If those pledged to Senator Kennedy won a majority, he received all of the state's electoral votes.

From time to time the concept of the Electoral College has been under attack and changes suggested. These attacks center primarily on the fact that the state's electoral votes are awarded on a winner-take-all basis. For instance, President Kennedy won all sixteen of New Jersey's electoral votes even though he had won the state by a narrow margin of less than 23,000 votes out of over 2,600,00 cast. Many people who favor a change in the nature of the Electoral College urge that the votes be awarded proportionately. Critics also argue that too much emphasis is placed on the heavily populated states.

There is some criticism also of the constitutional provision that if no candidate has a clear majority in the Electoral College "then from the persons having the highest numbers, not exceeding three, on the list of those voted for as President, the House of Representatives shall choose immediately by ballot, the President; but in choosing the President, the votes shall be taken by states, the representatives from each state having one vote." In recent elections, a variety of third-party candidates for President have been entered in the hope of preventing one of the major party candidates from gaining a majority, thereby allowing the House of Representatives to select the President. This has not happened because the two-party system is sufficiently strong to withstand these third-party movements.

Despite these criticisms, from a practical point of view there is little likelihood that there will be any constitutional changes in the near future that will alter the basic structure of the Electoral College.

Even though the national government does possess certain broad and specific power, the bulk of the election process lies within the individual states. First let us determine how the states organize to conduct elections. The pattern varies, of course, from state to state. Generally, however, the Secretary of State is charged with over-all responsibility for the conduct of elections within the state. His office makes the official canvass of the vote and certifies the winning candidate. He receives the official records of the campaign and election, especially financial reports of campaign expenditures. He also is responsible for the election calendar, determining when nominating petitions are to be in, when primaries are to be held, and in general attending to the myriad of details involved in running elections.

It is at the county level, or in some cases at the city level, that election lists are prepared and maintained. County boards of elections, county supervisors of elections, or county clerks are responsible for the actual conduct of registration and elections. These officials often have wide discretion within the state laws. For instance, they may decide whether to have registration offices outside the county office building or whether to have extra hours for registration. This can make a great difference in how many citizens are registered.

County officials must see that correct ballots are printed and distributed to the election precincts; they maintain, store, and deliver the voting machines. They appoint precinct election judges and other election-day officials. Usually the law requires that these election officials represent both major parties and that the Democratic and Republican parties have the opportunity to be represented in every election precinct.

Second, let us examine some of the specific details of our election laws. These laws deal with matters of registration, residence, age, nomination, ballots used, size of precincts, absentee balloting, time polls are open, and literally thousands of details required to keep our machinery in operation. Unfortunately, we can consider here only a few of the more important of these details.

Residence. In order to qualify as a voter, a person must reside in his state for a specific period of time. Recently there has been a trend among the states to lower the requirement. Twelve states now permit a person to vote after six-months residency in the state. Thirty-five states still require a year of residency, and three states require two years. All states have local residence requirements of varying degrees, usually ninety days in the county within the state and thirty days in the election district in which the vote is to be cast.

There is no real argument over the need for some kind of residence requirement to combat fraud and to allow people to become familiar with the issues and candidates. But in a nation where it is officially estimated that more than 20 million adults move each year, it is quite clear that this high degree of mobility does prevent some citizens from having the opportunity to vote. Reliable estimates indicate that 12 million would-be-voters in 1960 lost their vote because they could not meet state residence requirements. It seems likely that nearly 15 million citizens were similarly disfranchised in 1964.

In recent years some states have recognized that residence requirements should be minimal for voting for President. In fifteen states now, new residents who have been in the state for at least thirty days may cast a special ballot limited to the candidates for President and Vice-President. Seven states allow persons who move away to vote by absentee ballot for President if they are unable to qualify to vote in the state to which they have moved.

Registration. Forty-eight states require voters to register. There is a wide variety of procedures followed in order to register, but in every case the obligation falls upon the individual. He must make the effort. Registration may be permanent or it may be required that a person register for every general election. Even if registration is called permanent, a citizen must vote regularly or his registration is canceled and he must then take the trouble of reregistering. In some states, a person can register any time during the year except just prior to elections, when the books are closed to allow the election officials to prepare their records for the election. In other states, registration occurs only at stated times. Registration systems and practices are used in some parts of the country to discourage people from voting. This is particularly true in the South, where some registration offi-

AMERICAN POLITICS AND GOVERNMENT

cials do not wish to see Negroes register to vote. Federal laws, however, now allow the federal government, through the Department of Justice, to take steps to see that these discriminatory practices are ended. The Johnson administration is pledged to use the full national power to end these discriminatory practices against the Negro. Even if there is no discrimination, registration laws can make it difficult for a citizen to participate.

Absentee Balloting and Registration. Most states allow citizens who are going to be away on election day or who are physically unable to get to the polls to vote by applying for an absentee ballot. Some states allow citizens to register absentee also. Again, the process is cumbersome and it undoubtedly discourages some people from voting.

Each of the fifty states, however, has enacted a military absentee registration and voting system which is much simpler than the laws governing civilian absentee voting.

Form and Nature of the Ballot. The kind of ballot used also varies from state to state. Essentially, there are two ballots—machine or paper, but the continuing trend is toward the use of voting machines. At the present time, about 60 per cent of the vote is cast on machines. Ballots, be they machine or paper, can be organized in different ways. In some states the ballot is so organized that it is easy for the voter to vote the straight ticket; that is, for all the candidates of one party. He either pulls one lever on a machine or checks one box on the ballot and that automatically registers a vote for all the candidates of the party checked. Because the number of officials to be elected varies from state to state, the size of the ballot does also. A recent ballot in a midwestern state measured 2,414 square inches and contained 246 names. Many ballots contain not only names of candidates to be chosen but also highly involved public questions or state constitutional amendments. Because all of this can be highly confusing to the voter, there is some trend toward the short ballot; that is, reducing the number of names on the ballot and the number of public questions to be voted on in any given election.

In this brief discussion of some of the highlights of the electoral process, I hope that some impression has been gained of the magnitude of the process and its great diversity. Despite the shortcomings that have been chronicled, the American electoral process is a genuine tribute to the integrity of the system and the inherent interest of the American people in their government.

11 INTEREST GROUPS IN THE AMERICAN POLITICAL SYSTEM

Earl Latham

In 1835, Alexis de Tocqueville, a great French student of the American culture, said, "In no country in the world has the principle of association been more successfully used or applied to a greater multitude of objects than in America." That was 130 years ago, but what was true then is true today. In 1961 an American political scientist, the late V. O. Key, pointed out that a prominent place must be given to the activities of private organizations if one is to understand the American political system, for these associations constitute links of communication between the citizen and the government.

It is tempting to regard these statements as the decisive, if not the final, word about the activity of organized groups in the American society. Interest groups are free associations. They serve important political ends. Who should not cherish institutions that flower from a natural right of association, private organizations which are free of governmental control and therefore serve to check the tyrannies of class, party, and police? Certainly one of the distinctions between open and free societies, on the one hand, and the dictatorships of the twentieth century, on the other, is precisely their difference of attitude toward private associations. These associations thrive in the lands of the free. They die in the jails and concentration camps of dictators.

But other visitors from abroad and other students of American politics have thought that freedom of private association in America has incurred certain results that are less than admirable. André Siegfried in 1925 said that groups formed by private interest had become the true political parties in the United States and they constituted the core of political influence. He deplored what he thought he saw. Twenty years after Siegfried, an English professor of politics said that the city of Washington was full of special pleaders for private organizations and their activity, called "lobbying," was a major national and local enterprise. And he deplored what he thought *he* saw.

In view of this diversity of opinion, I should like to consider three questions. What are these private organizations? What do they actually do? What purpose do they serve in the American political system?

First, then, what are these organizations that feature the American culture? One of the difficulties in judging them is a failure of vocabulary. Phrases like "interest groups," "pressure groups," "private organizations," and "lobbies" are often used interchangeably, whereas care should be taken to separate their meanings.

Not all groups have direct political significance. For example, all people eight feet tall constitute a "group" in a statistical sense. To sociologists, the family is a primary group, to economists, investors are a group. Now, giants, fathers, and stockholders all have something in common within their respective categories, a something that can be called an "interest." Thus they may be regarded as interest groups. They may have some indirect political significance when parties and public officials voluntarily take their interests into account.

But interest groups can acquire direct political signifi-cance when they become political actors, when they actively try to influence the course of public policy, when *they* work to put favorable statutes into law or attempt to persuade officeholders to exercise their au-thorities for the benefit of the group.

Interest groups that are organized for action of this kind are thought of as pressure groups, and it is these that have direct political significance. The interest they promote may be a very material one, and the prizes they seek may be tangible goods, like increases in the mini-mum wage or high tariffs. Or the interests promoted by pressure groups may be intangible and symbolic, like the restoration of prayers in the public schools, an ob-servance which the U.S. Supreme Court recently held violated the American principle of separation of church and state. Labor unions and associations of manufactur-ers are interest groups when they are bargaining with each other over wages and hours; they are pressure groups when they try to influence the content of legisla-tion. An organization called Protestants United for the Separation of Church and State is a pressure group when it works to prevent the restoration of prayers in the pub-lic schools.

There are literally thousands of interest groups in the United States that promote material and symbolic goals and can become pressure groups when they work to influence the exercise of the public power.

Not only is their number large but the variety of their interests, as one can gather from a few of their titles, is great. There is an American Dog Food Institute, an American Goat Society, and an International Baby Chick Association. There is a National Flying Farmers Association and a National Horseshoe Pitchers Associa-tion. And a United States Federation of Amateur Roller

Skaters and a Society of Roller Skating Teachers of America. There is also a League for Less Noise.

It is worth repeating that not all the groups in this great number of busy organizations are politically relevant, because not all have political interests. Most of the time they are busy with internal affairs—with meetings, the elections of officers, discussions, resolutions, speeches, and reports. But they cease to be merely interest groups when they move into the political domain. When they work to achieve some political result, they become pressure groups, although their principal activity may be distant from government and politics.

A case in point is the American Medical Association, the principal professional association of physicians in the United States. It may be said of the AMA that it is an interest group when it concerns itself with standards of medical practice within the profession or with the dissemination of news about medical research to the membership. In the congressional elections of 1950, however, the association taxed the membership $25 each, created thereby a fund of several million dollars, and spent it to influence the election of congressmen opposed to the creation of a national governmental program of health insurance.

Not all interest groups are pressure groups, then, although all interest groups may become pressure groups when the occasion arises.

There are pressure groups, however, that maintain permanent offices in Washington because they have extensive interests and a continuing concern for legislation in Congress. Although anyone who goes to Washington on a single trip to try to persuade a congressman may be thought of as a "lobbyist," this term is usually reserved for the spokesmen for those pressure groups that maintain permanent offices in Washington. They aré the villains in a familiar and false stereotype of the political process in the United States. According to André Siegfried, they were to be found "at every turn, formulating new laws, overseeing the wording of the text, and controlling votes in Congress."

This is a wild exaggeration of what the spokesmen for private interest actually do, but, before we deal with that question, let us add a word of summary about them. Tocqueville was quite right—and still is—about the rich plurality of private associations through which Americans achieve personal and social satisfactions. The right of private associations is one of the fundamental rights in an open democratic system, and this right is enormously enjoyed in the United States. Most private associations are not politically relevant. Many do, however, undertake to influence legislation or otherwise affect the courses of governmental policy. And scores of them maintain permanent offices in Washington. They are very active in behalf of their memberships and they would certainly like to have it believed that they formulate new laws and control votes in Congress. They do occasionally get what they want, but this is far different from supposing that they pull all the strings of influence and Congress dances.

We come then to the second question: If Congress is not the stage for puppet masters of private interest, what is it that private organizations actually do when they act as pressure groups? Let us imagine a scheme or model of the procedure by which a public policy is formed and becomes a law. In this model, we can define the stages at which energetic representation of the interests of private organizations becomes important and may be influential. The first stage is the political party convention.

It is a commonplace to say that the national political parties in the United States are neither disciplined nor

146

doctrinaire, as parties abroad normally are. Instead, the national parties tend to be loosely bound associations of interest groups that cooperate with each other in the conduct of nominations and elections to federal office. Some of these groups, even within the same party, have incompatible interests. The platforms of the national parties tend to be a compromise of these interests. Spokesmen for private associations appear at the national conventions of the parties every four years and work to influence the terms of these compromises. Thus the National Association of Real Estate Boards may press for resolutions in the party platform that are favorable to private housing. Labor union officials will want promises of more social welfare and less labor regulation. The American Farm Bureau Federation may ask to be heard on agricultural programs. Representatives of ethnic groups will urge the adoption of foreign-policy planks that favor the concern they feel about affairs in the Middle East or in eastern Europe. Negro organizations will want strong resolutions on civil rights.

2 The second stage in the model of procedure for making public policy is the national election. During the convention proceedings and the election that follows, spokesmen for groups with a mass membership will try to lead the mass action at the polls that they suggest they can command. They will participate in the campaign by organizing rallies, making speeches, collecting money, and propagandizing in the press and on radio and television for candidates of their choice. Although it can happen that the election results do go in the direction in which effort was stressed, there is no guarantee that the leadership of any mass organization can deliver the support of its membership at the polls. In 1950 the labor unions of Ohio, with the support of labor unions outside the state, launched a tremendous drive to prevent the

147

re-election to the Senate of Robert A. Taft, who was thought by them to symbolize a philosophy of conservative reaction. Senator Taft nevertheless was re-elected by a large margin over a somewhat inept rival.

Pressure groups have also been successful in the support of political candidates. In the congressional elections of 1958, labor unions through independent political organizations helped to elect 126 members of the House of Representatives. In 1959 the unions opposed the enactment of the Labor-Management Reporting and Disclosure Bill which laid certain regulations on labor unions. The bill passed, but of the 126 members of the House of Representatives who had received financial aid from unions in the campaign of 1958, 116 opposed the bill, and only 8 supported it.

The third stage is the enactment of legislation, and it is here that pressure groups make concentrated and sustained efforts. The most formal and public method of persuasion is special pleading before the committee of Congress which has jurisdiction over the bill. The committee appearance is highly important because congressional committees are virtually little legislatures. Although a committee recommendation will not always guarantee passage of a bill, the refusal of a committee to recommend a bill almost always defeats it.

Besides appearing at committee hearings, pressure groups employ other more indirect and informal methods of influence. Congressmen often receive personal appeals from pressure group spokesmen or from notables who have been induced to "say a word." Congressmen and their wives will be flattered by invitations to social functions. Letter-writing campaigns may be stimulated among the constituents of the congressmen. Half a century ago, bribes and threats were not unknown, but these methods have long since come to be regarded as too gross and ineffective. The typical pressure group agent today is more likely to be a smooth, plausible, charming, intelligent, and solicitous expert in special pleading, armed with charts and other information, bent upon influence through smiling and insistent persuasion. It was a piece of culpable crudity for gas and oil interests in 1957 to attempt to make a contribution of $5,000 to the campaign expenses of Senator Case of South Dakota. His public exposure of the matter brought to a halt official action on a bill which gas and oil interests had wished to see adopted.

So open is the American political system that some foreign countries also operate as pressure groups for policies in which they are interested. The formal representation of foreign interests is, of course, provided through the embassies and ministries, but sometimes foreign pressure group activity functions out of the public view. The head of a Caribbean country provided vacations for the family of the chairman of a congressional committee with jurisdiction over sugar quotas. The leader of a large Asian country admonished members of his own legislature against acting as pressure points in the American Congress on matters of foreign aid. When the Department of State was considering a cut in the foreign aid allotment of one of the European countries, its ambassador in the United States appealed for help to congressmen of the same religious faith whom he had cultivated at luncheons and dinners.

The fourth stage in the model is the administrative stage. Congress provides an important focus for the concentration of the energies of pressure groups but so does the executive establishment and, to a more limited degree, the judiciary. The federal government maintains vast programs of expenditure for welfare and other social services and for military goods. Government con-

149

tracts for these goods and services are a not unimportant element in the economic system. The contracting agencies of the government, then, are centers for the concentration of pressures for tangible goods.

The competition for these tangible goods can sometimes involve highly placed administrative officials and members of Congress. The award of a contract for certain experimental aircraft to the General Dynamics Corporation in Texas instead of to the Boeing Corporation in the state of Washington recently created a controversy which drew into its vortex Cabinet officials and members of the United States Senate. Because top administrative officers are often drawn from the business world, they occasionally become entangled in a conflict of the public and the private interest, and the exposure of these occasional conflicts results in the resignation of the officials involved.

In the federal administrative system there are at least a dozen important regulatory agencies which are virtually independent of both the Congress and the President. Statutes of Congress, like the Administrative Procedure Act of 1946, regulate the procedures of these agencies so as to prevent bias and to protect the commissioners from pressure by private interests. Occasionally, representatives of business enterprise, in seeking special favor for their clients, have trespassed beyond the limits which the law sets upon influence. In 1957, one of the commissioners of the agency that grants licenses to operate television stations was discovered to have been financially compromised with an applicant appearing before him. The commissioner had to leave his office.

Similar examples of discreditable behavior by pressure group operators and by government officials could be cited in every country of the world. What is remarkable about the American system is that even though access by all the people to the officials of the government is freer and easier than it is anywhere else, the instances of sacrifice of public ethics are few.

5   Adjudication is the fifth stage in our model, and here the role of pressure groups is so narrowly contained that it might not even be supposed that they have one. The procedures of the courts are austere, and they are controlled by a jurisprudence of ancient rituals. They leave little room for improvising and none for direct manipulation. The judges are impervious to irregular approaches and invulnerable to imposition.

The courts do not institute the litigation they judge, but pressure groups may do so. Campaigns of litigation by religious and ethnic groups in the last thirty years have succeeded enormously in providing the Supreme Court with opportunities to enlarge religious and racial freedoms. A religious sect called Jehovah's Witnesses conducted a campaign of litigation in the 1930s and 1940s that produced a dozen key cases in the Supreme Court. A leading Negro organization, the National Association for the Advancement of Colored People, began a campaign of litigation in the 1930s that reached a stunning climax in 1954 when the Supreme Court held that the segregation of races in the public schools was a violation of the Constitution. These groups did not produce the decisions that favored their membership, but they did supply the Supreme Court with cases that advanced the law in the directions the Court had indicated it was willing to go.

There are two articles of belief about the activity of pressure groups that their spokesmen would like to cultivate but which empirical evidence does not fully support. First, the assumption is widespread that pressure groups are effective manipulators of public opinions which then turn the course of official events. But the number of people without any opinions at all even after a massive campaign of propaganda is discouragingly large. It may well be wondered whether the result justifies the effort. Second, it is an assumption of the leaders of pressure groups that their memberships support them in a solid unity, but empirical evidence shows that this is almost never the case. The officialdom of a private organization identifies itself with the goals it proclaims, but the commitment of the membership tends to diminish by the distance it stands from the center.

The image of self presented by pressure group spokesmen is often honored by uncritical acceptance, but it is frequently false. It is a willful or careless caricature of the fact to say that pressure groups get laws passed, see to it that they are applied, and control the votes of congressmen. Pressure groups exist. In fact they abound in the American political system. At their best they constitute links between the citizen and a large and sometimes impersonal government. At less than their best, they may distort a congressman's perception of public opinion, because they are special pleaders and because not all interests enjoy the same degree of organized group organization—that of consumers, for example. But there is plenty of law to control and punish outright venality and corruption, and a popular will to enforce it. The very number of the private organizations, adversary to each other, permits the congressman to discount offsetting claims. For important interests that may lack private promotion, there is public regulation to protect them, as in the example of the pure food and drug laws, laws governing weights and measures, laws against misrepresentation in advertising, and the like.

We come then to the third and last question. What function in the American political system do the interest and pressure groups perform? They perform a role which the nature of the political system makes inevitable. These groups exist not because Americans are more sociable than are people in other cultures (although they may be) nor because they are more self-seeking than people in other cultures (for they certainly are not).

Pressure groups exist because political power in the United States is divided between the federal government and the states, and, within each of these jurisdictions, it is further divided among the three branches of the government. There is no institutional arrangement for the concentration of these separated and decentralized powers. All members of Congress are elected from geographical areas of more or less narrow compass. No members of Congress represent the nation at large; yet there are great national interests that overflow the boundaries of the states and the congressional districts.

Normally these interests of tangible resources and ideology (what we might call functional interests) should find representation in the political parties, which *are* national in scope. But, as we have seen, American parties are not disciplined parties in the European sense, and the President sometimes cannot command the support in Congress of members of his own party. This circumstance provides scope for pressure group activity, and may even make it necessary. It provides scope because a congressman normally depends for re-election upon his own efforts and not those of a national party. He looks, therefore, beyond his own party for aid at the polls and for guidance in policy in some matters after he is elected. The pressure group may even be a necessity because it fills the need for the representation of functional interests as well as those of territorial localities.

The growth of pressure groups has actually created two systems of representation in the United States which mesh with and supplement each other—the geographical and the functional. The first is formal and the second is informal. An understanding of the principle of political representation in the United States must take these elements into account.

Interest and pressure groups in America are not to be condemned but controlled. Toward the end of the eighteenth century, James Madison, one of the framers of the Constitution, said that the "regulation of these various and conflicting interests forms the principal task of modern legislation." It is *still* a task of statesmanship to balance the universal right of free private association with the interest the public has in maintaining the integrity of the legislative and administrative processes.

12 PUBLIC OPINION

Douglass Cater

Communication is fundamental in the American system of government. Each day in Washington hundreds of thousands of words are spoken, tens of dozens of events occur. The press and other communication media perform the arduous task of sorting out and assigning priorities to these words and events. This capacity to choose with speed and brevity which events command widespread attention and which go unnoticed constitutes a power far more formidable than the purely editorial preferences of the press.

Communication, of course, is essential to every government, even the closed totalitarian system; however, there are important differences. In the Soviet Union, news is treated as a prepackaged product to be distributed or withheld, blown up or minimized according to the specification of the political leaders. By frank definition of the Communists, news is an instrument of government and the party for the education of the people.

In the British parliamentary system, the press does not play so large a daily role as in America. The Prime Minister and his Cabinet colleagues are obliged to report initially to the House of Commons, which is by ancient understanding the "embodiment" of the nation. Reporters are accustomed to serve as bystanders, recording and commentating on the two-way discourse within the official government.

In Washington, reporters are accustomed to a more intimate role. Unofficial communication between the executive and legislative branches of government—and within each branch—goes on regularly through the press, often in advance of official communication. Few policies of consequence are launched without the prior briefing of the press. Here, more than in any other major capital, the reporter accepts and even asserts the right to keep government informed about itself. He expects access to policy-making at every stage of the process.

The reasons for this intimacy are found deep in the constitutional ordering of power. Because ours is a government of "separated institutions sharing powers," there is need for constant communication if the wheels of policy are to mesh at all. Yet none of the holders of power designated by the Constitution would be satisfied to rely solely on a reporting system beholden to any other. The press, having its independence buttressed by private ownership as well as by constitutional mandate, must help serve this intelligence function.

The role of communication, however, does not stop there. Because power is fragmented in the American government, public opinion is called on more regularly than elsewhere to act as arbiter among the competing policies and politicians. Programs can live or die depending on whether they attract enough attention to build a favorable consensus among interested publics.

This has led to development of further unofficial apparatus for communicating public opinion back to Washington. Politicians pride themselves on their ability to maintain contact with the thinking of their constituents. But they have come to pay increasing heed to other methods for registering public opinion. There are the various polling organizations which claim to employ scientific methods for sampling public attitudes on a particular issue. There are also a variety of special interest groups in Washington which maintain their own private communication systems for alerting particular publics and eliciting responses that can be heard by the policy-makers.

The need for communication—grown increasingly urgent as government has grown big—has thrust the reporter into a role for which he is not altogether qualified. In theory, nothing guarantees that his definition of what is news will fix proper priorities among the important events of government. In practice, the priorities of the press can often be decisive, even reshaping the priorities of government itself. The men involved in politics at the higher levels develop acute sensitivity to the interplay between the reality and the image, between policy formulation and the publicizing of it. It has led to what might be called government by publicity in which a continuing preoccupation of the policy-makers is with the making of the news.

In no other major capital does the reporter have quite this political role. Patrick O'Donovan, former Washington correspondent for the *London Observer,* once commented:

> Most strangers are astonished by the power of the American and, more particularly, the Washington press. It fulfills an almost constitutional function. And it works with a seriousness and responsibility which —even though it may lack the luxuries of style—cannot be matched in Britain today....

Communication has developed into a massive and complex industry in Washington. The old stereotype of

157

the reporter as a seedy character operating with a hunch and a hangover no longer fits the corps of craftsmen, numbering upward of twelve hundred, who serve the high consumption needs of a highly specialized business. News is sought out, transmitted, packaged, and delivered in many different ways.

The backbone of the industry and, to a certain extent, its central nervous system are the giant wire services with a labor force large enough to monitor every major news outlet in the Capital and to maintain a steady outgoing flow of words. The wire-service employee scarcely conforms to old-fashioned notions of the reporter as one who each twenty-four hours dictates a first draft of history. He is rather the bucket boy for a never-ending stream of news that may be scooped up any hour of day or night and poured into print by the far-flung distributors.

Another sizable contingent of the Washington press corps is composed of the "localizers" of the news. They bear daily testament that the United States has become a world power whose interests are still heavily provincial. These reporters view Washington through the eyes of Dubuque, Iowa, or Kalamazoo, Michigan, or Nashville, Tennessee. They work as one-man vigilantes or as members of large bureaus specializing in perspectives from Maine to Texas.

There are the Washington bureaus of the big city dailies and the chain papers—highly varied operations ranging from the princely state maintained by *The New York Times* to the one- and two-man outposts of the Denver *Post* and the Providence *Journal*. These reporters are the most direct spiritual heirs of the long tradition of the Washington correspondent. They, more than the rest, provide the warp and woof of reporting.

Other reporters view the Washington scene from different perspectives. Reporters for the news weeklies such as *Time* or *Newsweek*—artisans on a different type of assembly line from the wire services—track down the primary components necessary to give a factual shape and color to the week's events. Other components—style, polish, "meaning"—are added further along the assembly line, in the skyscraper workshops of New York.

The Washington bureaus of magazines like *The Saturday Evening Post, Look,* and *The Reporter* concentrate on digging into the background of the news. Reporters for radio and television scan the horizon with restless radarscopes in search of news in shapes that can be heard and seen. Syndicated columnists, the most independent of the news merchants, batter the barricades for their "inside" news purveyed on at least a thrice-weekly basis and ranging in content from foreign policy to freight rates.

A trade press, in considerable numbers, sifts the capital city for the particular nuggets that will be of value to the organized interest groups keeping a relentless vigil over the government.

The syndicated columnist has been a peculiar development of American journalism. The packaged output of a single journalist may be distributed to millions of readers through newspapers having diametrically opposite editorial views. It has made the Washington columnist a formidable figure. Walter Lippmann, probably the most eminent columnist, has for three decades examined the confused fragments of daily events with a clear, perceptive intellect and is read and often quoted by heads of government the world over. Other columnists, both liberal and conservative, provide regular fare for politicians and public alike. Radio and, more recently, television also feature prominent Washington

159

news commentators who stimulate public discussion of the political events.

Finally, as Washington has grown into a capital city with the eyes of the world focused on it, the representatives of the foreign press have become an important contingent. Dozens of reporters from newspapers, radio, and television abroad are headquartered in the National Press Building alongside reporters from United States publications and broadcast media. Others reside in New York where they can cover the business of the United Nations, but they commute to Washington to cover important events.

Once we recognize the role of the press, we can better assess the arrangements that have evolved to maintain relations between government and the press in Washington. Starting at the White House, there has been vast change since the time when Woodrow Wilson, asserting that "news is the atmosphere of public affairs," inaugurated the regular presidential news conference. Today, the news conference has grown from an intimate gathering into a mammoth ceremony simultaneously shared with the viewing public. The press serves as a constant consort during a President's working day and is in attendance whenever he travels. Press deadlines play a large part in setting the schedule of a President's responses to the events crowding in on him. Many critics within and without government are appalled by this relationship. They argue that it encourages a President to speak offhandedly about matters of great moment, that he is hustled by routines not of his own choosing. The ready reply is that a President has no choice. If he values his leadership, he must play front and center stage in the drama of government. Otherwise, rival actors in Congress and elsewhere are eager to claim the spotlight.

Similar dispute rages over congressional dealings with the press. The legislators have increasingly resorted to their investigative power as an instrument of influence in Washington. The accusation is made that many of these investigations are staged simply to attract the mass media. Any reporter who has covered the hearings on Capitol Hill is aware of this orientation. The committee chairman displays skill in the techniques and timing of news, for inquiry is often paced to gather the maximum harvest of headlines.

The victims particularly grow irate when they witness these spectaculars in Congress. But we must note that the congressmen are affected by the same publicity compulsions as the President. Generating news is an important way to assert their own order of priorities. In this way they hope to capture the attention not merely of the general public but of Congress itself.

Another arrangement for generating news arouses continuing concern in Washington. It involves the subterranean channel of the "leak," which flows most actively during the periods when government is involved in crisis. As domestic or foreign trouble deepens, the reader is aware of a peculiar change in the news he receives. He continues to be informed about what policy-makers are contemplating but there is no indication of the origin of this information. The reporter has made himself a party to a conspiracy by which he engages in compulsory plagiarism. He reports official attitudes as if he had made them up himself.

Critics charge that the practice of cloaking the news provides an inducement to irresponsibility. When we permit the official to pass along information that he does not have to endorse publicly, we tempt those who seek to use news as a propaganda weapon. When we allow

161

the press to report without attribution, we permit the more sensationalist members to add their own special twist. The veteran attender of background conferences can cite many instances of both varieties of news fabrication.

Again, the realist finds it impossible to join forces with the prohibitionists who would abolish the practice. He recognizes that leakage serves a necessary function if communication is to be kept up during crisis periods. If handled in a responsible way, cloaked news can help prevent the orgy of wild rumor that occurs when official government spokesmen grow silent.

Communication between government and the public goes on in ways other than through the press. A President must devote considerable attention to establishing direct contact with the people. Franklin D. Roosevelt was first to exploit the potential of radio by his use of the "fireside chat" to discuss matters that he deemed worthy of public attention. Harry S Truman first escorted a television audience on a tour of the White House. Dwight D. Eisenhower carried this further by holding a simulated Cabinet meeting before the cameras. Soon after entering office, John F. Kennedy allowed the cameras to come into his office on occasion to watch the President informally at work. Lyndon B. Johnson shows a recognition that he, too, has found ways of direct communication. His use of television during the 1964 campaign was both extensive and effective.

President Kennedy once explained to a reporter, "The Presidency is an office which in a sense is shared by all the people." Although few would disagree with this generally, critics differ strongly with some methods of sharing this high office that create a false sense of intimacy about the governing process. When carried too far, it can make leadership into play acting and tempt the public to regard the President's job as less awesome than it really is. The President and other politicians find that it is no easy matter to communicate effectively in this age of mass communication.

Public opinion in America is not a monolithic whole spreading out from Washington. There are publics that listen and publics that must be listened to. They group and regroup in varying combinations. The politicians can never be entirely certain of the depth or duration of public opinion. Polls provide a clue. Three decades ago, when pollstering first became a discipline, the jargon about "image" and "trend analysis" invaded Washington. Additional experience has proved that polling has its limitations. Public opinion can be manipulated by which questions are presented to the public and in what fashion. Public opinion—or, rather, the opinion of certain publics—can be stimulated by skilled public relations experts who are seeking to accomplish their special purposes in Washington. There is still need for the politicians to decide when they must lead rather than follow public opinion.

No cry resounds more regularly in Washington than that someone is attempting to "manage the news." To judge from the outraged protests, one might suppose that the information about government should somehow flow by natural processes until its confluence with the great sea of public opinion. Actually, news is a commodity which involves anxious managerial concern all along the way.

The continuing debate between government and the press has not been much advanced by doctrinaire arguments. Too many zealous spokesmen for the public's "right to know" sound as if all government's business should be conducted in the newspaper headlines. Too many in government who decry the "irresponsibility" of the press are prone to judge news less for accuracy than for personal embarrassment. Neither concept has much relevance to the workaday world of the Washington correspondent.

Still, a more realistic assessment of the managerial problems of news does raise troublesome dilemmas. Man has come a long way since that distant time when, by projecting a series of photographs at a certain speed, the illusion of movement was created for the human eye, giving birth to the magic of the motion-picture industry. Today, much is known about creating illusions in the minds of people. Politicians faced with intractable problems are constantly tempted to employ the publicity resources of government to project images that do not correspond to reality.

The most glaring example of such image-making was provided by the late Senator Joseph McCarthy, Republican of Wisconsin. McCarthy was a demagogue of the mass media. Unlike earlier types, he was not proficient in the stump speech or the impassioned filibuster. Rather, he was a master at creating headlines—in timing his pseudo news to distract a nationwide audience over a prolonged period. By publicity, he built political power that permitted him, until he was felled by his own weapons, to disrupt the important business of government. Although McCarthyism has passed on, its basic evil—the cynical use of communication for deception rather than enlightenment—still crops up in Congress and elsewhere.

The dilemma of news management has acquired an extra dimension with the effort to add "national security" to the criteria by which news is to be judged. During active wartime, the government set the standards for semivoluntary censorship of the press. Now, during a permanent condition of cold war, there is great difficulty in defining the proper limits of what is news.

Our three postwar Presidents before Johnson worried publicly about the leakage of security information to the press. Truman once claimed that "95 per cent of our secret information has been published by newspapers and slick magazines." Eisenhower told a press conference in 1955, "For some two years and three months I have been plagued by inexplicable undiscovered leaks in this Government." But Kennedy carried the argument a bit further when, soon after the failure of the Bay of Pigs invasion, he addressed the publishers' association and declared, "If the press is waiting for a declaration of war before it imposes the self-discipline of combat conditions, then I can only say that no war ever posed a greater threat to our security." Kennedy argued that, while passing judgment on a story's news value, editors must also decide whether its publication would be in "the Nation's interest."

The attempt to articulate dogmas about the handling of "the news" can be a self-defeating proposition. A free press and a purposeful government are destined to be involved in war of sorts. What the protagonists should always be seeking is not total disarmament but a measure of understanding on weapons control.

Foreign visitors are often baffled by the conspicuous role of communication in Washington as well as the constant preoccupation of government officialdom with its processes. No other capital is quite so engaged. Hearing only the noise and surface confusion, the observer may be inclined to suspect that publicity has grown out of bounds in the American system.

Yet, there are fundamental reasons for this. Under our constitutional separations, the President has no means of ordering Congress to obey him; Congress cannot command the President. Other power is vested in state governments, and, finally, a substantial chunk of power reposes in the citizenry. For government requires the constant flow of communication to evolve policies and carry out programs.

13 INTERGOVERNMENTAL RELATIONS

Roscoe C. Martin

It is axiomatic that democratic government adapts itself continually to the needs of the society it serves. As a corollary, the society that prevails in a given country will determine, or at least profoundly influence, the kind of government found there. Six characteristic features of American society have particular significance in intergovernmental relations. First is the technological revolution, which, although stemming from the industrial revolution, has stamped current scientific developments with a character all its own. A concomitant feature is the increasingly rapid trend toward industrialization. A third is the trend toward urbanization, which in some ways is a consequence of the previous features but at the same time has a life of its own. Yet a fourth feature inheres in basic population changes, notably of growth and mobility.

These (and other like) developments give rise to a fifth feature: America grows increasingly more complex and varied in social structure, in economic organization and practice, in patterns of family life, in politics, in short, in the things that describe the way of life of a people. The sixth and final feature, which in a sense summarizes what has been said so far, attaches to the simple but overwhelming fact of change and, more especially, the rapidity, even the violence, with which change takes place.

Rocket launchings have become commonplace in the face of the widely advertised moonshot project; a smallish Caribbean island, but recently held to be of limited importance, achieves worldwide renown almost overnight as the seedbed of communism in this hemisphere; the "revolution of rising expectations" comes home in a domestic revolution which shakes the Republic as it has not been shaken for a hundred years. More faithfully and fully than any other characteristics, complexity, diversity, and change reflect the nature of the contemporary American scene.

It is therefore not strange that the society just described has produced an equally complex, varied, and frenetic government. Government in the United States is complicated almost beyond human comprehension. There are more than 91,000 units of government, employing more than 8,000,000 civil servants. At the top of the heap is the national government, with 2,400,000 civilian employees and an annual budget which runs in the neighborhood of $100 billion. Next are the fifty states, which vary greatly in size, population, economic resources, and governmental activity. All other units (91,185 in 1962) are local governments, a category including counties, municipalities, townships, school districts, and special districts. These governments are "local" only in the sense that they are substate. They vary dramatically when measured by almost any criterion one may wish to invoke—size, area, resources, functions performed, numbers employed, money spent. They run the gamut from a New England town, which with a population of twenty-five pursues few activities, to New York City, which by any standard is one of the half-dozen biggest, most active, and most important governments in the United States.

If these many and varied governments were constrained to operate each within a fixed geographic limit, in strict accordance with a legal definition of powers, and without reference to other governments, the American people would be poorly governed indeed; only an artificial or mechanical discharge of public duties could result from such strait-laced action. Fortunately, no such strict construction policy prevails. On the contrary, there is a vigorous discourse permanently in progress among governments, constantly seeking ways to pool their resources, improve their methods, share their burdens, and spread their responsibilities. The result is a nationwide network of intergovernmental relations whose purpose it is to make government operational in the domain of action.[1]

These intergovernment relations are of the widest conceivable variety. Some are legal, some extralegal; some are formal, others quite informal; some are defined in geographic terms, others emphasize functions; some are local, others are regional, and a few are nationwide in scope; some result from simple political understandings, others involve very technical administrative arrangements.

Because of their complexity and their diversity, the problem of classifying relations among governments is a difficult one. Yet, some system of classification must be employed if the subject is to be made manageable. Intergovernmental relations may be classified as vertical—that is, relations between governments on different levels (federal–state, state–local) and horizontal—that is, relations among governments at the same level (state–state, city–city, and so on). Some relations are vertical and

1 Intergovernmental relations normally reflect a search for ways of intergovernmental cooperation. The two terms are used interchangeably in this essay.

horizontal at the same time. We shall speak here of vertical and horizontal relations as two separate categories, noting at the same time that they are not mutually exclusive.

International relations are also intergovernmental relations. The United Nations, its various specialized agencies, and such regional associations as NATO and OAS are likewise based on a system of intergovernmental relations. Here we shall confine our examination of the term to the continental United States, where we shall discover intergovernmental relations more than enough to keep us busy.

VERTICAL RELATIONS

The up-and-down relations among governments in the United States are dominated by the federal system, essentially an arrangement for the division of public powers between different levels of government. The federal system is found in a number of countries—in Canada, Australia, and New Zealand, to name but three—but its progenitor, as federalism is known today, was the American system. Here the national government and the fifty states operate within the framework of a federal partnership which is delineated in the Constitution of the United States. Reduced to its simplest terms, the purpose of the framers of the Constitution was that the national government should be vested with powers in areas beyond the competence of the states—foreign affairs, the conduct of war, coinage, interstate commerce, and the like—while the states should be left with residual powers over all things not delegated to the central government.

The framers did what they reasonably could to describe the field of action perceived for the national government and thereby make explicit the relations between the nation and the states. This effort was foredoomed to failure, for changing times and circumstances made modifications necessary in federal–state relations. Fortunately, the Constitution was sufficiently flexible to permit accommodation to changing needs; such phrases as "interstate commerce," with reference to the national power to regulate; "the general welfare," with relation to the power to levy taxes and make expenditures; and "necessary and proper," which made it possible for the Congress to augment its list of granted powers through addition of certain "implied" powers, not only permitted but also required interpretation.

The federal system by definition rests on the concept of a continuing relationship between central and state (or provincial) governments. By necessity, these relationships are close, complex, and constantly changing. There are those who maintain that Supreme Court decisions handed down during the last ten years have wrought nothing less than a revolution in the federal system—that is, in federal–state relations.

However that may be, practice began to give meaning to the federal system with the adoption of the Constitution, and federalism today ramifies throughout the domain of national and state action. Thus one may speak of functional federalism as it relates to federal–state relations in such important fields of activity as education, health, and the construction and maintenance of public roads. One may also speak of financial federalism as it concerns the labyrinth of arrangements by which federal–state activities are financed. Functional and financial federalism necessitate a host of operational relations; hence we may identify an administrative federalism. Because many operational relations involve professional people—doctors, lawyers, and the like—we may also think in terms of professional federalism.

Many important federal–state programs generate consumer interest and support at both levels; and, when these consumers organize on a national basis to support a total program, as they frequently do, it is not far-fetched to speak of a cliental federalism. Finally, the federal system has resulted in the growth of an extra-legal political organization geared to its requirements, and one is therefore constrained to recognize a political federalism. Thus the legal federalism outlined in the Constitution has permeated the practice of federal–state relations in every walk of public life.

At another level is found an important set of vertical relations between each state and its local government— between New York, for example, and its 3,800 local units. The state is the legal reservoir from which each and every one of these governments sprang, and in legal theory the state has complete control over the local governments within its border. In actuality, the local governments enjoy many safeguards and many rights at the hands of the state constitution, although these guarantees vary widely from state to state. There is a wide gulf between what is legally possible and what is politically feasible, for it is not to be doubted that local governments are stronger in point of political power than they are in point of legal theory. The case may be argued, indeed, that a nascent federalism prevails within the state, with state–local relations generally comparable to those which exist between the national government and the states.

In operational terms, the relations between the local units and the states are many and close. Local governments are created by and draw their legal powers from the state. The terms by which they may expand, enter into agreements with other governments, and go out of business are fixed by state law. Such state departments as education, health, and highways, to name but three of many, maintain close working relations with various local governments. Among such relations are state aid to local enterprises and, as a consequence of state aid, state participation in such matters as the drawing of plans, the setting of standards, and supervision and inspection. The supplying of state personnel to local departments, chiefly in technical areas, is by no means uncommon.

In yet another direction, one finds active and growing relations between the federal government and local governments, particularly the cities. These relations are closest in such fields as urban renewal and airport construction, where mutuality of interest and concern has produced lively federal–local programs. In many cases, the relations between the national government and the localities (principally the municipalities) are direct, though occasionally the state will assert its interest and declare itself a partner to the proceedings. Something approaching a three-way federalism embracing all levels of government may be said to exist.

Enough has been said to indicate something of the lively relations that prevail among governments at different levels in the United States, but not enough, it should be added quickly, to have afforded anything approaching an adequate description of those relations. It is clear that the federal system as defined in the Constitution is one thing, while the federal system in everyday life is something different and something more. So also for the legal doctrine of state sovereignty over local governments, which would find hard going but for the accommodations that have been worked out in practice. The service of vertical intergovernmental relations is that they bring governments at different levels into working

(as distinguished from legal) relationships with one another. They supply the flesh and blood which make
American government a physiological being rather than
an anatomical specimen.

HORIZONTAL RELATIONS

On horizontal relations—that is, relations between or
among governments at the same level—there is an almost infinite variety. First, the states have found it ad-
vantageous to enter into arrangements among themselves. Sometimes these arrangements are of a political
—one might say an almost fraternal—nature, as when
the state governors come together in their annual conference for consideration of subjects of common interest.
There is a trend toward increasing seriousness in this
national meeting, whose tone is distinctly more business-
like than it was, say, thirty years ago. There is also a
national federation of state legislators, which counts
among its major contributions the promotion of interstate relations through creation in many states of commissions on interstate cooperation. The parent organization, the Council of State Governments (COSGO), has
devoted a considerable share of its energies over the last
quarter-century to the furtherance of interstate relations
and, particularly, to the pooling of state resources for
joint attacks on common problems.

In a more formal way, varying numbers of states
(from two up) have entered into agreements covering
a wide spectrum of subjects. Sometimes such agreements
are consummated through an interstate compact, which
has been described as a treaty entered upon by two or
more states and which must be approved by the Congress. One such compact, involving the states of New
York, New Jersey, and Connecticut, created the Inter-

state Sanitation Commission to abate pollution in the waters of the New York harbor area. There are many such compacts, and they cover a wide variety of subjects. A few have drawn in all the states as signatories, but most deal with local or regional problems and involve not more than half a dozen states. Not all agreements among states rest on interstate compacts; some rely on nothing more formal than parallel statutes passed by the legislatures of the participating states or on executive agreements entered into by the governors. The Interstate Commission on the Delaware River Basin (INCODEL), which for many years worked toward the abatement of water pollution in the Delaware Valley, was a significant interstate undertaking that rested on informal agreement.

In interlocal relations, the intellectual traveler enters into a forest which is so tangled that he may lose his way. There are, it will be recalled, 91,185 units of local government (1962 figure), running from somewhat more than 3,000 counties to almost 35,000 school districts. These governments practice the widest conceivable variety of relationships among themselves—city–city, county–county, city–county, city(or county)–district; this is not a complete listing, but it is sufficient to indicate the possibilities. There are literally thousands of these interlocal arrangements, although to date no one has undertaken a census of them. Los Angeles County alone in 1961 provided a total of 1,278 contract services to seventy-three cities.

Many observers have identified eight to ten varieties of interlocal relations, and a recent study listed sixteen. Chief among these were informal agreements (covering, for example, voluntary cooperation among neighboring fire departments), advisory councils of government, service contracts, agreements to transfer functions to a larger unit (frequently the county), special districts, metropolitan government, and regional agencies. The classification of some of these devices as interlocal may be questioned; the criterion is whether or not the arrangement rests on agreement among the governments involved. To illustrate the point, the Metropolitan Water District of Southern California is a special district which answers this description; although it is a creation of state law, the district was established at the behest of local governments to serve local needs.

As in the case of interstate cooperation, there are several organizations which have as a major purpose the promotion of cooperation among local governments. Thus most of the states have leagues of municipalities, which in turn are organized into a federation called the American Municipal Association. The National Association of Counties (NACO), while emphasizing the importance of the role to be played by the urban county, likewise stresses interlocal cooperation. A movement recently launched jointly by the International City Managers' Association and the American Association of School Administrators seeks to introduce an element of reason into the relations between the cities and the urban school districts. These are but illustrative of the many efforts afoot to rationalize the labyrinthine relations among local governments.

DETERRENTS TO INTERGOVERNMENTAL RELATIONS

Of the many obstacles which discourage efforts at cooperation among governments, half a dozen stand out. The first arises from the fact that it is not always easy to delineate a program in terms that will elicit cooperative efforts by two or more governments. Further, the concerns of interested governments in a particular problem may not be equal, or equally advanced, at a given time. Resources also may vary so widely as to make it difficult to arrive at a formula for cooperation. From considerations of program, then, arrangements for cooperation among governments are sometimes difficult to make. Second, there is the related fact that each government is presumed by law to be adequate to the program responsibilities vested in it. The law often does not perceive the importance of cooperation and, hence, does not make provision for it. The path of intergovernmental cooperation is a rocky one at best.

A third obstacle inheres in the ancient but still vigorously championed doctrine of states' rights. The doctrine had an honorable parentage in an honest difference of opinion concerning the scope of action designated for the federal government as compared with that reserved to the states; but recently it has served chiefly as the rallying point for those who would obstruct national action in the name of state sovereignty. There are some areas in which certain states do not concede the need for or the desirability of public action and, hence, are not amenable to proposals for cooperative endeavor. Civil rights is one such area, perhaps the outstanding one. Fourth is the absence of vigorous state leadership in the field of intergovernmental relations. The states have been slow both to avail themselves of the advantages inherent in intergovernmental arrangements and to authorize relations among their local governments. This reluctance has stemmed partly from adherence to states' rights and the resulting attitude of defensiveness, partly from the continued domination of the state legislature by rural elements wedded to the tradition of little government mentioned below, and partly from the fact that the states have not revealed notable resourcefulness or imagination in dealing with the problems of urbanism.

Fifth, at the local level there are twin doctrines which have adversely affected development of a habit of inter-local cooperation. One of these is the dogma of local (city and county) home rule, the other the tradition of "grass-roots" government. These combine to elevate local governments to the position of miniature sovereign states, to affirm the adequacy of local units to deal in-dividually with their problems, and, as a natural result, to downgrade the promise of cooperation with other governments. Sixth and finally, some problems lie out-side the scope of any local government, or any ready-to-hand concert of governments, and so languish for want of a spokesman either to identify an issue or to propose a course of action. This is true of the problems of metro-politan areas and of those of larger regions as well.

PROSPECTS FOR THE FUTURE

Notwithstanding these and similar obstacles, the prac-tice of intergovernmental cooperation is growing apace. There are many organizations which emphasize the promise of interstate and interlocal cooperation. It was only in the mid-fifties that the national government took formal cognizance of the subject, though of course that government had engaged in the practice of relations with both states and local units for a great many years. The (national) Commission on Intergovernmental Re-lations, appointed in 1953, published a weighty report (with extensive supporting documents) in 1955, and, since that date, there has been a lively and vocal interest in Washington in the subject. That interest culminated in the appointment in 1959 of an official and permanent Advisory Commission on Intergovernmental Relations. The Commission, which represents all levels of govern-ment, devotes the full time of its modest but competent staff to exploring the opportunities, improving the forms, and expanding the practice of intergovernmental relations. That the lessons of intergovernmental cooperation have not been lost on the national government's operating departments is attested by the interest shown in the subject by numerous federal agencies. The Housing and Home Finance Agency, as a single example, recently sponsored a study of interlocal cooperation in metropolitan areas.

Meanwhile, a number of state legislatures, observing the trend toward increased intergovernmental relations and sensitive to its promise, have passed acts specifically authorizing widespread cooperation among local units. Local governments, too, are exhibiting a lively interest in interlocal relations. The service contract continues to grow in popularity. In the decade since 1954, some ten voluntary councils of government have been formed to stimulate cooperative action in as many metropolitan areas. Metropolitan planning finds increasing favor; a recent national study produced information on 126 metropolitan planning agencies. In 1962, Nashville and Davidson County (Tennessee) went all the way and established a metropolitan government. In 1961, the governments of the Delaware Valley, in concert with the federal government, cooperated to establish the Delaware River Basin Commission for the management of the Basin's water resources.

It is clear that intergovernmental cooperation is in forward motion in the United States. More and more groups and organizations recognize the significance of such cooperation; what is more important, more and more governments avail themselves of the advantages inherent in collaborative effort. The rationale is simple and easily stated: There is no virtue in autonomy which may prove empty and high virtue in cooperative arrangements which multiply resources without sacrifice of essential freedom. The practice of intergovernmental cooperation breathes life into what often would otherwise be an empty, perhaps even a vain, enterprise. That it will continue to grow in scope and variety is not to be doubted.

14 STATE GOVERNMENT IN THE UNITED STATES

Robert S. Babcock

The foreign observer of American government, accustomed to headlines emanating from Washington, can be forgiven for assuming that most American government is national and centralized. But this is far from the truth. As originally conceived by the Constitution, the states of the United States were semisovereign and they delegated their authority to the central government in Washington. The Civil War presumably killed the notion that the states were sovereign bodies, capable of nullifying national action on their own account. And the national government, especially since Franklin Roosevelt's administration, has substantially increased its power. In spite of this, the states still govern in a wide range of fields, sometimes in harmony and cooperation with the federal government, sometimes independently and almost in defiance of the federal government. The doctrine of states' rights is still a potent political force. Part of the difficulty surrounding the solution to the problem of Negroes' civil liberties in this country stems from the resentment over federal intrusion into the state's traditional sphere of power and interest, an intrusion resented in some cases by people otherwise wholly disposed to aid the Negro.

There are now fifty states. Alaska and Hawaii, pre-

viously territories, were admitted as states in 1959, the
first new states since 1912. On admission, their individual state constitutions had to be approved by Congress, as well as by a popular referendum in those territories. Possibly someday other territories may become
states, although there is no immediate prospect of that
happening. Once admitted to the Union, each state is
legally equal, and each has two senators in the United
States Senate; but its number of congressmen depends
on its population, however, each state is entitled to at
least one representative.

Alaska exceeds 500,000 square miles; Texas is about
half that size. Rhode Island covers merely about 1,000
square miles. The most populous state is now California,
home of Hollywood, San Francisco, and Los Angeles,
with about 17 million people. It has just surpassed New
York, which was the most populous for more than a
century. Two of the states, Alaska and Nevada, have
populations as small as a quarter million.

The relation of these states to the federal government
is analogous to conditions in, for example, Brazil or
India or Canada. Unlike those countries, however, the
bulk of governmental power, as originally conceived in
the Constitution, was granted to the states. In the Constitution the powers of the federal government are
enumerated. The Tenth Amendment, adopted in 1791,
and for all practical purposes really a part of the original
Constitution, specifies: "The powers not delegated to
the United States by the Constitution, nor prohibited by
it to the States, are reserved to the States respectively, or
to the people." In other words, the powers of the federal
government are said to be "enumerated" and "delegated," with all the rest reserved to the states. Because
the actual list of enumerated powers is brief, although
couched in broad language, the powers reserved to the

states are theoretically vast. And for 150 years, at least until World War I and the Great Depression, the states did do most of the governing. Even today their role is considerable.

The expansion of the power of the federal government at the expense of the states resulted primarily from new interpretations of two of the clauses of the enumerated powers in the Constitution. Section 8 of Article I grants Congress the power "to regulate commerce with foreign nations, and among the several States. . . ." Until the New Deal the words "regulate commerce" among the several states were narrowly construed to mean in practice merely the control of interstate transportation. Since that time, because of Supreme Court interpretations and the obvious impossibility of any individual state being able to cope with the national problems of prosperity, agriculture, trade unions, and working conditions, the federal government has subsumed the broadest possible interpretation of that phrase, so that almost any commercial, industrial, or agricultural activity may be regulated by Congress.

The same section of the Constitution says "The Congress shall have Power . . . to pay the debts and provide for the common defence and general welfare of the United States. . . ." This is known as the "spending clause." As presently interpreted, Congress does *not* have the power to provide for the general welfare of the United States, but it may spend money for that purpose. In other words, Congress may grant money to the states for, let us say, welfare purposes, and place conditions on the expenditures of that money, including matching funds, which the states must meet or lose the money; however, Congress itself may not directly provide for the general welfare. Naturally, practically no state has ever turned down the federal grant-in-aid, no matter how stringent the conditions of the grant, for fear of losing the money. Both these clauses considerably undercut the powers of the states. But without them, solutions to most national problems would probably be impossible.

The current controversies in the United States about further federal aid to education or to health involve federal grants-in-aid and in many states are resented as further federal invasion of states' rights.

The internal structure of each of the fifty states is remarkably similar. Each has a governor. All but one have a two-house, or bicameral, legislature. None has adopted a parliamentary system of government, although there is nothing constitutionally preventing them from doing so. If, originally, the states were regarded as laboratories for experiment, on paper at least this has not happened. Yet each state does have its own peculiarities, mood, tradition, and history of partisan strife. This of course gives each one a special flavor and often develops individual characteristics and institutions. It is sometimes dangerous, therefore to generalize about them. A small, agricultural state in New England, like Vermont, is vastly different from the huge, lusty, arid, cattle and oil state of Texas.

Each state has a written constitution. Some of them are brief—6,000 words or less; others are long, wordy, ill-drawn and amended countless times. These are, however, the organic acts of each state from which the state government draws its powers or finds specific limitations to its actions. Every state requires a popular referendum for any amendment to its constitution. Some methods of amendment are easier than others, but the states ordinarily require an unusual majority of votes to amend a constitution.

Each constitution reflects the American doctrine of separation of powers; specifically, it sets up an executive, a legislature, and a separate judiciary, each, in theory, checking and balancing the other. In practice the doctrine of separation of powers has largely broken down, with the exception that the judiciary is everywhere independent. But increasingly the governor has been granted broader control over legislative matters. Each constitution contains a bill of rights, safeguarding the citizen against arbitrary governmental action and protecting minorities.

The governor in each state is modeled on the President. He is the chief executive and far and away the most important individual in the state. He is elected on a partisan ballot, as either a Republican or a Democrat; third parties are a decided rarity. His term of office is either two or four years. In one-party states—where the Democrats or the Republicans are in overwhelming majority—the governor is likely to represent one "wing" of his party.

Unlike any state legislator, and indeed unlike even a United States senator who is also elected at large in the state, the governor is regarded as having a special mandate from the entire state electorate, a mandate that often includes a legislative program. Although nominally possessing only a few legislative powers, the governor in fact is the chief legislator. He spends much of his time, therefore, working with his party or with his wing of the party trying to secure passage of his measures through the session of the legislature. While in office he is certainly the titular leader of his political party in his state.

To accomplish his program a governor uses all the weapons, both political and constitutional, that are available to him, in a fashion very like that of the President on the national scene. He uses such political patronage—the awarding of jobs—as may be available. As the state's spokesman and figurehead, he has special access to the press, radio, and TV, which he fully uses to accomplish his aims. And he administers a large bureaucracy, far larger than most private businesses, engaged in numerous diverse activities. Indeed, the governorship is like the Presidency in miniature, except the governor has no foreign affairs or defense matters to concern himself with.

A governor of any of the large states—New York, California, Texas, Ohio, Michigan, Pennsylvania, or Illinois—is automatically a potential presidential candidate because a governorship is superb training ground for the Presidency, and a governor of a large state can be presumed to carry that state in an election, with its accompanying large Electoral College vote. Only a United States senator, whose constituency also is a complete state, is in a remotely comparable position.

With the exception of one state, Nebraska, all states have faithfully copied the two-house, or bicameral, legislature. The upper house is invariably known as the Senate. The lower house is usually called the House of Representatives; and members are known as either senators or representatives, or sometimes as assemblymen. The basis of representation is usually on population in one of the houses and on geography in the other. No members are elected at large. A member's constituency is usually a county or a subdivision of a county. In some states there are multimember constituencies.

The boundary lines of these electoral divisions either are found in the state constitution or were established by the legislature. Most state constitutions demand that the boundaries be redrawn after each federal decennial census.

In fact, however, there are gross inequities in representation or apportionment in almost all the states, either in one or in both houses. Most state legislatures have failed to redraw electoral boundary lines, in spite of any constitutional injunction to do so. The vast shifts of population in the United States in the past several decades, from the rural areas to the cities, and subsequently from the cities to the suburbs, have made the old boundary lines meaningless.

Until 1962 the United States Supreme Court had held that any remedy for malapportionment was political, not judicial; that is, no court could have jurisdiction, but the remedy had to be by the legislature itself through political pressure. In a momentous decision, which will have political repercussions for years to come, the Supreme Court reversed itself. It held that malapportionment was in violation of that clause in the Fourteenth Amendment which says, "No state may deny to any person the equal protection of the laws." Suits to reapportion state legislatures are now pending in more than three-fourths of the states. At this writing the result is anything but clear. The courts may hold that both houses of state legislatures should adhere as nearly as possible to the principle of one man, one vote. Or perhaps the courts will permit some modification of this principle to allow representation of geography in at least one of the houses. At any rate, state representation is in an upheaval at the moment.

The Senate is usually the smaller body, averaging about 40 members; the lower house is usually larger, averaging perhaps 100 members. There is, however, wide variation. The smallest house has 35 members, the largest 399.

The term of office is usually two years, although in about half of the states the term for senators is four years. In all but a few large states, the legislature meets only every two years, customarily in January. In some states there is a constitutional limitation to the length of session, ninety days, for example. In others, the session usually lasts four to six months. Except for the large states, like New York, in which legislators meet annually and receive high salaries, the pay of the members is on a very modest per diem. For these members service in the state legislature is an amateur, part-time performance. In all states except Nebraska the members are elected on a partisan ballot, as either Republicans or Democrats; but party label, especially in the very small constituencies, may count for far less than local popularity.

In all but the very large states, therefore, where political party organization is strong, state legislatures are relatively independent bodies and are not nearly so tightly controlled or organized as in the Congress in Washington. But they do adopt a biennial budget, set taxes, and enact laws in all their wide diversity.

Contrary to what many Americans believe, most court cases in the United States are state, not federal, cases. Most crimes are state crimes; most suits are in state courts. President Kennedy's assassin, had he lived, would have been tried for murder in a Texas state court. The Anglo-American common law has been adopted in practically every state; therefore state, not federal, courts hear the bulk of civil and criminal cases.

In every city and county and local government unit, there are trial courts, established by state law. Often there are specialized courts for traffic cases, for family relations, for juveniles, for probate, and so forth. In every state there is a state supreme court, which, in most cases, is the ultimate appellate body. Between the trial courts and the supreme court there are usually intermediate appellate courts, designed to reduce the work load of the supreme court and to allow only the most important cases to filter through to the top. Generally, appeals are permitted only on questions of law, not of fact.

The caliber of these courts and the method of choosing the judges vary considerably from state to state. In spite of occasional scandals, the general integrity of the bench remains high. Americans will often tolerate peccadilloes in their legislators which they would not permit in their judges.

The supreme court judges ordinarily are appointed by the governor, sometimes on recommendation of the bench and the bar. Most judges, however, are elected, some for short terms, some for long terms, usually from a county or a city as the constituency. In a majority of cases they are elected on a partisan ballot as either Democrats or Republicans. Very little has come under more serious criticism than our method of choosing judges, but no change has yet found any considerable favor.

Generally speaking, a case may go from a state court to a federal court only in two circumstances: If citizens suing each other are residents of different states, the case may be tried in a federal court. Or if a "federal question" arises—that is, if the constitutionality under the *federal* Constitution of a state law or city ordinance is challenged—the case could go to a federal court.

Besides administering justice, what else does a state do? It builds and maintains highways and roads. The hundreds of thousands of miles of roads—certainly the highest per capita anywhere in the world, because of the tremendous American reliance on the automobile—are not in a strict sense federal roads. How they are constructed and maintained is a graphic illustration of our intergovernmental relations. Roads are built and maintained by local government units—towns, cities, counties; roads are also built and maintained by the states.

Local roads are often subsidized by grants from the state governments to local communities, on complex and varying formulas. On the other hand, the federal government grants funds to the states for the construction but not the maintenance of roads. Most of these grants are on a fifty-fifty basis: the state meets half the cost, but the federal government gives the specifications. However, on the vast new interstate system, consisting of 41,000 miles of four- and six-lane highways with no intersections or crossings, the federal government is paying 90 per cent of the cost of construction and setting the specifications. This national highway is scheduled for completion in 1970. It affects every state, not always equally, and some states are ahead of others on percentage of completion.

The federal government is financing this road by a tax on gasoline of four cents per gallon. The states finance their road costs by gasoline taxes, usually from five cents to eight cents per gallon, and by automobile license fees. The 65 million automobiles are issued registration plates by the states, and each state plate often advertises its own virtues with a short phrase, like "Illinois, Land of Lincoln."

A principal function performed by the states is the care and treatment of society's unfortunates. States, and sometimes local communities, not the federal government, establish hospitals for the mentally ill. The hopeless mental cases—idiots, mongoloids, and so on—are cared for in state institutions, some of which are exceedingly well directed, and others poorly managed. With the exception of certain federal prisons holding violators of federal law—smuggling, counterfeiting, income-tax evasion, and the like—it is the states that regulate the penal institutions for the punishment and correction of most criminals. The states or local communities also manage the specialized correctional institutions, such as those for delinquent children. Obviously the quality of these institutions varies considerably from state to state; however, wealthy states, like New York, often set the standards for the others to try to meet.

In the broader field of general public welfare, there has evolved a more complex intergovernmental relationship between the state and the federal government, with the federal government's powers depending on both the spending clause and the interstate commerce clause.

Social Security, a compulsory retirement and life insurance plan which covers possibly 80 per cent of all workers, is solely a federal function. The federal government also grants funds to the states, on a complex matching formula, for people reaching sixty-five who are in need and not covered by Social Security. The states determine who is eligible for this old age assistance, and the monthly payment, and they administer the program. A similar arrangement exists for the care of dependent and neglected children. The poor and needy adults under the age of sixty-five are, in most states, the responsibility of local government units, sometimes with state financial assistance.

With the exception of the military academies, there are practically no federal schools or colleges. Education at all levels is the responsibility initially of local governments and secondarily of the states themselves. One of the great current controversies is the extent to which the federal government should assist education. Traditionally, Americans have felt strongly that the control of elementary and secondary schools must be left in the hands of locally elected school boards, independent of even other local governmental units. Elementary and secondary education for all is generally free, being paid for by local taxes on property and by state aid. Because some local districts are poor and others wealthy, the demand for equality of educational opportunity has long since forced almost every state to make grants of money to local school districts, in a variety of formulas. Indeed a considerable portion of state expenditures is for aid to education. For this purpose each state has a state director of education, who often has power to set local standards. It is the inequality of educational opportunity in different states, especially involving schools in largely Negro districts, that has led to demands for federal aid to education, in various forms.

Every state also maintains at least one state university, and many states have established several, with different specialties; California is the leader in this field. The hopeful theory is that no qualified student should be denied a college education because of lack of funds. The states bear the brunt of this expense. The federal funds so far available are principally for aid in construction of buildings and for a vastly expanding research program, particularly in the physical sciences, as a response to the challenge of Sputnik.

Within the states, there is an incredibly complex mixture of local governmental units, including counties, cities, towns, villages, special districts, and other municipalities. All of them have been created by the state, through its legislature. Their geographical boundaries and powers have been set by state statute. Usually they have been created at the request of local citizens of the area involved, but they are the legal creatures of the state.

In political fact, however, once established these units are rarely abolished and their boundary lines are almost never changed. Legislatures almost invariably require local consent for their abolition, and such is the loyalty built up in the local units that consent is rarely granted. Each state has granted many local powers to these political units, especially in the fields of education, poor relief, health, and general police power. Consequently, although the state is nominally and legally the superior body, there is often friction and divided authority between the state and its local political units. One of the perplexing and undecided problems in American government is how properly to divide that power and responsibility. The problem usually comes to a head over the question of the amount and kind of state financial grants to the local governments.

Not all state law is alike. From state to state provisions may vary considerably on different matters. It is easier in some states, for example, to charter insurance companies, and the maximum rate of bank loans may be higher in some states than in others. The restrictions on labor union activity may be more or less rigid. State laws vary on the sale or use of intoxicating beverages. As a temperance device, sixteen states held a monopoly on the sale of liquor. Divorce laws also vary considerably. In some states, divorce is exceedingly difficult. Reno, Nevada, has made a name for itself because of the ease with which divorce may be granted—merely six weeks is required to establish oneself as a resident of Nevada and then only very loose grounds for divorce action are required. (If the divorcee returns to the state of original residence, an awkward legal tangle may readily ensue; the United States Supreme Court has only recently clarified this in part.)

To meet these and similar problems, a number of official and semiofficial means of cooperation have arisen among the states, including formal agreements which may have to be approved by Congress if they are "interstate compacts." For example, many states are members of an interstate probation and parole compact, which permits a prisoner, released from prison in one state on probation, to return to his home state under the supervision of the receiving state's probation officers. Twenty-two states are members of an interstate oil compact designed to control oil production and conservation by mutual action. Many states, sharing a common river valley, have made interstate compacts for flood control and water supply purposes. Any list of informal cooperative agreements would be large indeed.

States finance themselves in many ways. The principal source of income of the federal government is a progressive income tax on persons and on corporations. The principal source of income of all local government throughout the United States is a tax on real estate and personal property. The states, in a large part precluded from these sources of revenue, have looked to taxes on the retail sales of particular commodities and either on broad retail sales taxes or on personal income taxes, or combinations of them.

Almost all the states derive considerable revenue from retail sales taxes on such commodities as liquor, beer, cigarettes, and other tobacco products—the so-called "sin" taxes. About two-thirds of the states enact an income tax on individual persons and on corporations. The rates invariably are much lower than those set by the federal government. About two-thirds of the states also enact some form of broad retail sales tax on the sale of all commodities (with the exemption of certain necessities usually described as food and medicines and fuel). The rates are usually about 3 per cent. Which is the more equitable form of taxation and which is the more profitable is frequently a matter of political debate in many states. For each state is in a continual contest with the others in attempts to attract industry or tourists into their borders.

The federal government has exclusive jurisdiction over foreign relations and defense. It also has increasing jurisdiction over those domestic economic matters that can be solved only nationally. But in a real sense the function of the states is to try to provide for domestic tranquility. So the states, or their creatures, handle law and order, the day-to-day business of maintaining roads, caring for the poor and rehabilitating the unfortunate, providing direction and many of the funds for education, and in general trying to see to it that the good life is possible for the citizen.

15 LOCAL GOVERNMENT

Charles R. Adrian

Local government in the United States stems from an ancient heritage. It can trace some of its antecedents to the city-states of ancient Greece, the direct democracy of the wandering tribes of prehistoric Germany, and the feudal system of Anglo-Saxon England. It has borrowed ideas about the structure of government from a variety of other sources, too. For example, the initiative and referendum, which are devices for direct democracy, may be traced in part to old Swiss practices. The use of general-act charters, which I shall discuss in a moment, is to some degree a heritage from the French Revolution. Some of the complex relationships between local governments and the state and national governments are the result of the federal system of government that was established at the time of the American War for Independence and in the United States Constitution of 1787.

Whatever their historic backgrounds, local governments in the United States are creatures of the regional, or *state,* governments rather than of the national government. They are created by action of state law or by the state constitutions directly and bear no direct legal relationship to the United States government itself. The national government often deals with local governments, of course, but in doing so it treats them either as agencies of the states or as if they were something on the order of private corporations.

In their relationships with one another, local governments generally are on a par; therefore, interlocal relations require negotiations between two or more officials of equal power and importance. A city government, for example, does not regard itself as subordinate to a county government, although the two may have elaborate patterns of relationships and many points of administrative contact. In legal theory, a unit of American local government is a corporation created by government. At one time in Anglo-American history, there was no specific difference between a private and a public corporation. A sharp distinction has gradually developed between the two, but the concept of the municipality as a corporation is still clear in law.

Because of the subordinate legal status of local governments in the United States, it is necessary for the courts to decide questions of whether or not a particular local government has the power to perform a certain function in a certain way. As creatures of state government, they can do only those things authorized by the state government, and only in an authorized manner. In general, in the absence of clear authority, the rule is that the local government does not possess a particular power, and any doubtful activity will be classified as illegal.

The traditional rule holds that the municipal corporation possesses only those powers granted to it expressly, those necessarily or fairly implied in the powers expressly granted, or those essential to the accomplishment of the declared objects and purposes of the corporation. This rule can be vexing to local officials, for it requires them to go to court whenever a citizen of the community makes a legal challenge of local powers. This is particularly likely to happen whenever a new function is undertaken by local governments or whenever a new procedure is established for an existing function. It is especially likely to be a problem for the large cities of the country, where most policy innovations originate.

But the rule also serves as one of the many safeguards of democracy that Americans customarily build into their political system. The rule makes it relatively easy for state government officials to retain control or at least a check on local governments. It permits any citizen or group of citizens to challenge a proposed public policy, and it constantly reminds local officials that they must be sure of their right to govern before they seek to do so.

Every American city or village has, as its basis, a charter from the state government. The standard practice from colonial times until the middle of the nineteenth century was to grant a special charter to each city. It was drawn up by the legislature, although not always with the advice of local officials and citizens. Ordinarily a local vote of approval was not required before it was put into effect. This pattern had been the prevailing one in England in the days before the American War for Independence and it was the standard practice in all the colonies.

Obviously, the special-act charter permitted the legislature to give the community any form of government it wished. Gradually, the tendency of the legislature to impose its will on a particular community became a handicap that offset the natural advantage of the special-act charter as a device by which governmental structure could be tailor-made for the needs and wants of the people living within the boundaries of a particular local government. Beginning about 1850, some states began to outlaw special-act charters or to allow them only after due notice had been given to residents of the local government that the legislature was considering changes in the city charter and after an open hearing at which interested persons and groups could testify. This modification of the special-act charter approach is still used in a number of states and is essentially similar to the current practice in Great Britain. The major drawback to this approach has been that legislatures have often been unwilling to support a plan that has the effect of restricting their own powers.

The idea of the general-act charter that replaced the special-act approach stems from some of the concepts of the French Revolution in the late eighteenth century. France, as it was reorganized after the fall of the monarchy, adopted a system of local government based on the *commune*. In all of the land, the basic unit of local government was the same, except for the special circumstances of the metropolis, Paris.

The idea that the same form of government should be used for all cities of the state irrespective of size or local political circumstances was popular for a short time as a reform device in the United States. Its purpose was to reduce the influence of the legislatures over local political decisions.

In practice, the objective of a single general-act charter to apply to all communities in the state—the French plan—was not successful, in part because the courts gave a narrow interpretation to the meaning of a "general act," taking the view that any act which, on its surface, was a general act would be so accepted.

One of the responses to the abolition of special-act charters and widespread dissatisfaction with general-act charters was the use of optional charters. Under this system, each state government provided for a number of different plans of city government; that is, for various forms of government, any one of which could be adopted locally by popular referendum. A state might offer from three to as many as fourteen different basic charters, and local citizens could choose from among them. The actual powers of local government generally did not vary from one city to another, but the structure of the administrative system, the office of the chief executive, and the legislative branch ordinarily did. The legislature still controlled the basic framework, however, and all amendments to optional charters required legislative approval before they could go into effect.

Municipal home rule represented yet another, and still popular, attempt at local political autonomy. It was entirely an American development, involving a process under which a municipal corporation may frame, adopt, and amend a charter for its own government and may exercise all powers of local self-government, subject to the constitution and general laws of the state. The idea of municipal home rule was first developed in the middle of the nineteenth century. The system was an unusual one. It permitted municipal residents to elect the members of a charter commission. The commission then drew up a proposed charter for the community. This charter was voted on by the eligible voters; if approved by them, it would go into effect. Another important characteristic of municipal home rule was that all amendments to the local charter were to be proposed either by a charter commission, by the city council, or by some other local political body, and those proposed amendments would go into effect only if approved by a majority of the eligible voters expressing an opinion at the polls.

In 1964, home rule was provided for in the constitutions of twenty-three of the fifty states and was actually in use in cities in all but two of the states. In some states, home rule was authorized only for the large cities, because these were the local areas where the rules particularly needed to be fitted to specific local circumstances. In other states, however, most cities and villages could frame, adopt, and amend their own charters.

In practice, home rule has not given local communities a greater amount of legal power, but it has given them flexibility in meeting their problems and has minimized interference with local self-government.

It is not easy to discuss local government in the United States. There are many types; and no standard nomenclature exists. Terminology differs from state to state and an understanding of terms used must be based on local conditions.

The most common term for an urban area in the United States is *city*. This term is Latin in origin. In England, its application was restricted to cathedral towns, but in the United States it is commonly the normal term for a large urban place. It thus has in this country approximately the same meaning as does the British term *borough*. Borough is also used in the United States, although it is uncommon. It has legal status in five of the fifty states, but it is not used in any consistent fashion. A city does not, however, necessarily include all of the urbanized territory that is contiguous. Large urban areas, in the United States called metropolitan areas, commonly have many, in some cases hundreds, of cities and other local units within their boundaries.

The term *village* originally referred to a farm or a country house and the settlement that surrounded it, but in the United States today it usually means a small, essentially rural, trading center. The word is not consistently used, however, and in some states legally incorporated villages may be larger than some cities in the same state, and suburbs of tens of thousands may legally be villages. Furthermore, in some states rural trading areas are legally referred to as towns, although this term is also used in different ways in different states. The town in New England was originally a small trading area and the countryside surrounding it. Since colonial times it has been a legal unit of government, but today it is often equal to a city in size.

In much of the northern part of the United States there is a legal unit of local government known as the township. This most commonly covers an area six miles by six miles in size; that is, it is a unit of government based on an area determined by the surveyors of the American frontier for their convenience in describing land locations. It is thus rather arbitrary in size, but in some states it has become a major unit of local government.

The county, on the other hand, stems from a familiar unit of local government in medieval England. Historically, it has served as an administrative unit of the state government. In size, it has varied considerably throughout the country. In the Middle West, the dimensions of the county were determined roughly by the distance in all directions from the county seat that a horse and buggy could reasonably travel in a single day. In the South, where there were never any townships, the county has always been somewhat smaller in size. In the area west of the Missouri River, where population has always been quite sparse, except along the Pacific Coast, the county has been larger in size.

The number of local units of government in the United States has not remained the same through time. Although the number of counties has changed very little in the twentieth century, the number of cities and villages has increased by more than 1,000 in the period since the end of World War II. This has been largely a result of recent incorporations in the suburbs of metropolitan areas. Towns and townships, for example, have decreased in number in the last generation. The functions of local government are varied, complex, technical, and vastly greater in number and scope than they were in the nineteenth century. Even so, they are fewer than they are in many nations of the world.

Although there are some exceptions, American local governments generally do not engage in manufacturing, trade, or distribution enterprises. These activities are normally reserved for the private sphere of endeavor. Local governments do, however, perform almost every type of public protective and service activity. They have responsibility for protecting the public health, for police and fire protection, for garbage, rubbish, and sewage removal, for a variety of welfare activities, for the education of the vast majority of American children in the years between kindergarten and high school graduation, and for the ensuring of accurate weights and measures in shops and markets. They also have the task of providing dozens of different services: germ-free water supply, public transportation systems, the construction and maintenance of streets and sidewalks, street lighting, storm-water drainage, and others. Many local governments also perform functions which in other American cities are sometimes performed by private business: some manufacture and distribute electricity and gas; a few operate telephone systems, radio stations, and other enterprises; many operate wholesale produce markets, auditoriums, or buildings for group meetings. The variety is almost endless and the pattern of activities and functions is different in each city and county.

The typical metropolitan area in the United States contains a large number of local units of governments.

Frequently these units are too small to provide adequately for certain urban municipal services. As a result, the tendency has been to create special districts to provide of these services. The number of nonschool special districts in the United States approximately doubled between 1942 and 1962.

The structure of American local government is so complex and varied as to defy description in a lengthy book, much less in a brief essay. The basic traditions stem from those of Anglo-Saxon and medieval England. But the variety is great. In general, counties and rural units of government do not have a chief executive with great powers, and often they do not have a single chief executive of any kind. This decentralized pattern of decision-making stems from the days of the American frontier when governments performed relatively few functions and their officials were not trusted by the highly individualistic yeoman farmer who believed that whatever progress he made in clearing away the wilderness and gathering for himself some personal possessions would likely be the result of his own sweat and toil.

In the emerging American cities, the rural pattern was first imitated and throughout nearly all of the nineteenth century the weak-mayor plan prevailed. The mayor was weak in terms of administrative powers. The council, through committees, often participated in administrative activity, and municipal activities were primarily the traditional public safety responsibilities of medieval European cities. As America became urbanized and local government functions became more complex, an increasing need for effective administrative and political leadership developed; but the American urban public, echoing their rural ancestors, demanded that administrative actions be subject to the authorization, review, criticism, and modification of a popular assembly in the form of a city council. Similarly, as functions became more complex, the patronage system of personnel administration that Americans had found adequate and an effective protection against a domineering administrative class had to give way to a professionalized civil service; but Americans continued to oppose the development of a strong, aristocratic, and arrogant bureaucracy. This desire was so strong that Americans have almost carried it too far. That is, as the need for professional experts became manifest, there has been a problem in convincing these people that government service is prestigeful and important enough to devote themselves to it. Gradually, however, the old frontier fears have been overcome to the extent of permitting the recruitment of able civil servants to perform the complex functions of modern city government.

Toward the end of the nineteenth century, the strong-mayor plan began to be used in larger cities and is today the most common plan in cities of over half a million. It calls for a separately elected mayor, as in the weak-mayor plan, but it concentrates administrative powers and responsibilities in his hands. The council has gradually become smaller—often consisting of only five to ten members—and is generally made up of amateurs who meet only a few times a month and do not become involved in administrative detail.

In the twentieth century, two new and fundamentally American plans for city government have been developed. At the beginning of the century, the commission plan appeared. It called for the election of five or seven men, chosen from the city at large, who would act individually as heads of major agencies and collectively as the city council. The plan, by its very nature, contained several major defects and began to decline in popularity about the time of World War I. It was abandoned in many cities in favor of the council-manager plan, which is today the most popular single plan in the United States and is particularly common in the many suburbs that have been incorporated in the last twenty years.

The council-manager plan combines, in a happy manner, the American desires for both democracy and reliance on the expert. It calls for a city council of laymen who devote part time to their duties and represent the citizens of the community. They are responsible for public policy. The administration of that policy, the carrying out of its detailed application, is in the hands of civil servants who are chosen for their professional qualifications. The professional emphasis is carried even to the office of the chief executive, for the city manager is chosen (and sometimes dismissed) by a majority vote of the council. He need not be a member of a particular political party or faction, or even a resident of the city. In the ideal model, and most of the time in practice, he is chosen solely on the basis of his professional qualifications.

A manager today typically spends a lifetime in his chosen field, moving from one city to another as opportunities for advancement develop. He is responsible for all of the city's operations, but he is accountable to the council at all times, being subjected to interrogation and, sometimes, criticism by these elected representatives of the people. If his performance is regarded for any reason as unsatisfactory by a majority of the council, he can be summarily dismissed and another manager hired in his place. Today this plan, and the strong-mayor plan, are the principal forms of city government in the United States. They are being extended, although rather slowly, to urban counties, townships, and other units of local government.

At one time, political issues in the United States were

settled on the national, state, or local levels, or through a combination of efforts of representatives of these levels acting cooperatively in sharing decisions. But with the development of the suburban movement after World War I and, especially, after World War II, this approach became inadequate. As America became metropolitan-ized, rapidly expanding population came to live in an increasingly small portion of the total geographic area. But the American devotion to home rule and to the preservation of a sense of access to the decision-makers did not permit the emerging metropolitan areas to be consolidated under a single local government. Even if there were popular support for doing so, the problems would be enormous, for American cities have tended to grow along the main highways, creating a spider-web effect rather than one of urban expansion through the use of solid blocs of land.

Although many urban functions can be handled by either local or state governments, there are a number of problems that are specifically metropolitan-wide in char-acter and require cooperative effort on the part of doz-ens, perhaps hundreds, of local governments, as well as aid from two or more state governments and the na-tional government. Water supply, the preservation of streams in unpolluted condition, traffic-flow and public transportation systems, smoke, noise, and communicable-disease control, and coordinated and logical land-use practices, among other activities, all require some kind of cooperative approach which American metropolises find new, novel, controversial, and still highly experi-mental. State governments are increasingly providing assistance in meeting these problems, without usurping the local autonomy that Americans prize so highly.

As to the future of American local governments, it is probable that they will continue to operate much as they have in the past. Americans generally believe in gradual change and, despite the rapid urbanization of the country, it is probable that the pattern now prevailing in urban areas will be little changed from today. The principal differences between the future and the past will probably be found in the increasing dependence upon state and federal financial assistance to local governments and in the increasing degree to which state and federal agencies share in decision-making in local areas, particularly in matters where several local units of government are concerned with a single problem. The pattern of decision-making that is known as "cooperative federalism" is familiar and comfortable to Americans. It reserves an important sphere of policy-making for local decision-makers. Local governments have always been important to the American way of life. They will continue to be.

16 COMPARATIVE GOVERNMENT

Roy C. Macridis

From the days of Herodotus and Aristotle man has marveled at the diversity of political systems and governments, political values and beliefs, habits and institutions. What seems right in one political society seems wrong in another; institutions that are taken for granted in some parts of the world are flaunted elsewhere. In our times more than ever before diversity is the rule. Different systems, institutions, and values confront the student of contemporary society. More than one hundred nations are represented at the United Nations and each has its own peculiarities and political habits. "Human nature" seems to splinter into particular types and shapes when viewed in terms of political behavior and action.

This diversity is both a handicap and a challenge. We have before us a rich and diverse world to study and understand. We lack, however, the basic methods of natural science. We wish to generalize and to find regularities and laws that account for political behavior, yet we are confronted with such a fragmentation that no generalization can stand the test of empirical confirmation. We would like to explain the differences that separate modern democracy from a one-party system, but as soon as we try we throw up our hands in despair when we are faced with so many variables—climate, geography, the economy, personality, social classes, literacy, regional attachments, prior conditions that we call history, ideologies, even accidents—and they all account, some more and others less, for the character of a given political system. The most we can do at times is to test some ideas, but testing has neither the validity nor the certainty that the scientist commands in his laboratory. Controlled experiment is impossible in social science where we deal with human beings who in a sense *make* their own political environment and history.

When it comes to matters of policy and policy-making, what some call social engineering, the predicament is even more serious. A natural scientist can make a bomb; he can develop techniques to combat disease and can suggest ways and means to measure the yield of the soil. The test of his ability to do so is that ultimately what he does has a predictive certainty—the bomb will explode, the disease will be curbed, or crops will grow more abundantly. Social scientists still grope in ignorance and are uncertain of what causes what and what will produce what. The argument that is raging today in the United States about foreign aid is very much to the point—social scientists are unable to predict with any assurance what the impact of economic aid will be upon the recipient society, its values and institutions, and the rate of its development. Comparative study has not as yet yielded definite conclusions. We are still at the level of expediency and trial and error.

The public should not be too readily disappointed. Contemporary students are probing and studying political behavior in many lands, and we are beginning to develop, if nothing else, some of the basic intellectual tools of analysis and study. Comparison itself means, after all, the establishment of basic concepts, without which it cannot take place. Concepts are intellectual devices that help us define the *categories* in terms of which political systems can be identified and at the same time differentiated. They are yardsticks with which we can measure. As in all sciences, such yardsticks must have at least one characteristic—they must be abstract and general, that is, they must include as much of the actual political experience as is possible.

Until recently, political scientists remained faithful to what we might call the legal and formal institutions of a state—the constitution, the courts, the organization of the governmental powers, the formal requirements for elections or lack of same. Most systems were studied in those terms. Constitutions were carefully classified (rigid vs. flexible, written vs. unwritten) and governmental forms were classified as parliamentary, monarchical, presidential, despotic, authoritarian, totalitarian, and so forth. Very often, however, such an analysis is not helpful.

We tend, by putting too much emphasis on formal and constitutional arrangements, to forget the informal but often all-important aspects of political organization and process. What is the value of studying a constitution, for instance, when we know that it is only a façade behind which important economic groups control the political decisions? What is the purpose of studying the formal organization of government when we know that it is ineffective in some regions or vis-à-vis some groups or tribes? Comparative analysis therefore has made one important step toward the distinction between what we call formal arrangements and informal processes. Among the informal processes we now include the organization of power and influence in any given society. Power and influence stem often from nonpolitical factors such as wealth, birth, status, and the control of the media of communication and education. It is only when we take into consideration these informal aspects of social and political life that we can develop some new categories and concepts in the light of which we compare.

By connecting formal institutions and informal arrangement institutions we get an overview of a political system. It is a mechanism that can make widely enforceable and respected decisions. On the one hand, we have the informal elements—interests and social classes, economic demands and needs; on the other hand, we have the governmental machinery that makes decisions which are enforceable. Analytically, we have interest groups on the one side and the government on the other. The link between them is the political party. To paraphrase the famous words of a British political philosopher, the parties are today everywhere the buckle that binds the social interests and groups with the government. If we keep this basic definition in mind, we can view political systems in terms of three elements: interests, parties, and the government, that is, the executive, the legislatures, the courts, the administration.

We must also view political systems in terms of their stage of political development, otherwise we would be ignoring many of the new societies—the "developing" or "emerging" political systems. The distinction between "modern" and "underdeveloped" or "emerging" is not hard to make: Modern society can be differentiated from the underdeveloped or emerging societies in terms of political participation—interest articulation and what we might call a sense of community (consensus). In the emerging societies participation tends to be, at least in the beginning, very low. The peasants—the rural population in general—impoverished and illiterate, are not ready to participate in politics except through violent revolutionary movements that have no permanency and stability. At times they even resist participation and try to remain attached to their own village or community or tribe. There lies their first loyalty.

The same is generally true about interests: interest groups are few in underdeveloped societies. With the coming of economic development, the middle classes, the proletariat, and other social groups begin slowly to manifest themselves and to articulate their interests and seek their satisfaction. Political activity is often in the hands of a small group that has been playing a very important role in all national movements: the political leaders and the intellectuals. They suggest the ideas that arouse participation and involvement. They seek to bind these groups to new national symbols that will break down the indifferences and apathy of the past and will destroy the loyalties to tribes or regions. The intellectuals are today throughout the underdeveloped world the social and political engineers of the future. What ideas do they use? What images do they suggest? Where are they guiding their societies? We shall try to answer these questions.

Finally, the underdeveloped societies are in the process of community building. The effort of the intellectuals and the leaders is to create new ideas and suggest new symbols that will bring all the people together into a truly national community. This means an effort to develop shared symbols, ideas, and beliefs and to bind the citizens through them into one political community. In other words, many of the developing nations are going through a process that is similar to the breakdown of feudalism and the creation of organization in Europe in the centuries before the French Revolution.

Today's phenomenon is even more urgent. The niceties of democracy and individual rights are often forgotten in the process, just as religious toleration and individual rights often were forgotten in the Europe of

the seventeenth and eighteenth centuries. The new nations represent a specific stage of political development
and an entire branch of comparative politics is devoted
to their study and analysis.

It is in the developed and highly modernized nations
like England, France, the British former dominions, the
United States, Germany, and the Soviet Union that the
study of the three categories we suggested earlier—interest, party, and government—becomes more meaning-
ful. Here the study of parties, interests, and the governmental machinery yields important generalizations and
insights.

Political parties are, relatively speaking, newcomers
to the political scene. It was not until the middle of the
nineteenth century that they appeared with a national
organization and leadership. The extension of the fran-
chise, the demand for political participation, and the
requirement for responsibility of the governors to the
governed have made the parties the most significant institution of both democratic and totalitarian systems. In
all of them, the party or parties perform similar functions: they articulate interest; they provide for popular
support to the leaders; they provide a way by which the
mass of the electorate can exert pressure and hold the
leaders accountable.

Two-party systems, so prevalent among the Anglo-
Saxon countries but emerging now in France and West
Germany, tend to perform these functions better. They
not only express demands and interests but they also
provide supports without which no government, no
matter what the constitution, can exercise leadership
and make decisions. Multiparty systems which have been
the rule in Europe do not provide the same support.
By allowing every minority and every interest the possibility of becoming a party, they also blunt interest ar-

ticulation. Instead of general policy programs within which interests and groups seek a modus vivendi and reconcile their differences, multiparties account often for a highly diffused structure of interest representation which accentuates divisions. Nor do multiparty systems as a rule provide the support to the government needed for decision-making. They lead to coalition cabinets, account for political instability, and often lead to what the French call *immobilisme*.

It is particularly with regard to accountability that the differences between two-party or multiparty systems and one-party systems become noticeable. Granting that the one-party system—like that of the Soviet Union or of the many emerging nations such as India, Ghana, and others—can provide for articulation of various interests and for support to the government, it is hard to accept that they also provide for accountability. The one party often becomes a monopoly; it controls the media of communication and expression and does not allow for alternative leadership groups to come forth with new programs and new leaders. The electorate does not have the power to throw out the government by voting for a different party. Elections do not provide the opportunity of ultimate control, the only true hallmark of a democracy.

It may well be that one-party systems, Soviet or others, are only temporary steps leading to the development of two-party or multiparty societies; that with the development of political community the governing groups will feel secure enough to open up the electoral process to other contending groups. It may well be, in other words, that one-party systems are indispensable historically to create a political community in which the people participate and share common attitudes before they begin to exercise the ultimate prerogatives of choice and control. It is too early to tell.

Party structures are organically linked with the organization of the legislatures and the relationship between legislature and executive. Generally, two-party systems make easier a parliamentary majority, which in turn accounts for cabinet stability and leadership. Multi-party systems, generally, but not always, account for instability and a weak executive. There are exceptions to these rules. In the United States the two-party system has certain peculiarities that in essence resemble the French party system under the Fourth Republic. The parties are divided on regional and ideological grounds and do not have a clear-cut leadership. They lack discipline and common orientation. The American system gets its stability and leadership from the President, who is directly elected by the people and accountable directly to them, every four years.

No matter what the Congress does, the President cannot be forced out of office. He stands as a steward of the nation and his power in foreign-policy matters and as Commander-in-Chief are formidable. There are multi-party systems which provide for executive stability in a parliamentary setting. This is notably the case in Holland, Belgium, and the Scandinavian countries. Executive stability is attained because of a contract between political parties to support a given government, under a given program, for a given period of time. The discipline of the parties is great and their deputies are expected to respect the agreements and support the government.

Because of the emergence of political parties, and for a great many other reasons as well, parliaments and legislative assemblies throughout the world have weakened. The parties organized on a national basis provide leaders, define policy, articulate interests, and provide for a majority. Legislative action flows from the party. Legislatures are no longer deliberative bodies that make decisions. They have been becoming instruments through which the party majority legislates and governs. This is clearly the situation in England and may become so in France and Germany. It constitutes the general trend everywhere. It is clearly the case with all one-party systems where the party overshadows completely the legislative organs. The only exception to this generalization may well be the United States, where the members of the two parties organized in powerful legislative committees not only scrutinize actively every legislation but also originate their own measures, sometimes with the support but sometimes over the desire of the President. It is curious that the British continue to refer to parliamentary supremacy and mean today really cabinet government, but we in the United States talk about a presidential system when our Congress is far more powerful than the House of Commons or any other legislative body in the world.

There are still other reasons for the decline of Parliament, reasons that even the Congress of the United States has to reckon with. The complexity of social affairs, the urgency of decision-making, the role of the government in social and economic affairs and, finally, the need for political, social, and economic planning have called for administrative and governmental discretion and freedom in a number of areas.

The legislature is satisfied to set down general goals, leaving the task of implementation to the executive. The special knowledge needed for certain policies in foreign affairs and military matters is not shared by legislators. Therefore, the executive assumes more powers. The development of economic programs like the TVA or of foreign programs like the Peace Corps, for example, cannot be directed by the legislature.

In the nineteenth century, John Stuart Mill was the first to note this trend and to point out that legislatures are not fit to govern; their job is to control. Initiative tends to come more and more from the executive and the civil service. The linkage between parties and the executive makes this possible without endangering democracy. In most democracies today there is a direct connection between the people and the government through the political parties.

All democracies have become mass democracies; they all have plebiscitary elements; they all give room to personal leadership, that is, to the personality of the party leader. People vote for policies or against them, to be sure. But they also vote for or against a man. Again the sharpest difference between one-party and two- or multiparty systems is that in the former no contest is allowed, whereas in the latter, contest is free. In the last analysis, the popularity of a given leader can be assessed only in an open contest provided by the parliamentary systems of the Continent and England or the presidential system of the United States.

There are also many technical reasons for the ascendancy of the executive branch. A modern society needs trained civil servants to perform the vast array of technical, economic, and social tasks—welfare, pensions to veterans, preparation of the budget, collection of income taxes, operation of economic services (especially in the countries where some economic activities are nationalized), health, inspection, and, last but by no means least, defense. Millions of people in all modern societies are civil servants, with tenure, special skills, and special functions. Issues that were debated in the past have gradually become routine operations within all systems

—outside politics—performed by civil servants. Thus the executive branch becomes a vast bureaucratic machinery for the performance of service and the implementation of policy. Responsibility and accountability of the civil service become a problem which is far more difficult to solve than that of the accountability of the executive because the areas of operation in which civil servants are involved require competence and know-how to which day-to-day control cannot be applied by either the legislature or the political leadership.

Over and above the civil service, the cabinet in the parliamentary systems and the President's Office in the United States act as a staff for policy-making. They initiate legislation; prepare the budget to be submitted to Parliament or Congress; use the vast discretionary powers they have to carry out decided policies and bear alone the heavy burden of military decisions, a burden that with the advent of nuclear weapons has become staggering. At the very top, the executive has become a vast deliberative, policy-making, and planning agency, as well as the director of the civil service, the army, and the various specialized agencies and nationalized industries. Its job is to make policy to coordinate the activities of the various departments and to see to it that policy is properly implemented. It stands at the very apex of the political system coordinating economic and foreign policy and military strategy.

The executive branch is the brain in a vast nervous system; it requires information before it acts, intelligence in order to decide, and strength in order to carry out what has been decided. It is no wonder, therefore, that both the modern Cabinets and the Presidency under the presidential or quasi-presidential system have developed their own internal bureaucracy, their own staff and intelligence agencies, and a number of other organizations. Fifty years ago the President of the United States had one or two secretaries. Today there are scores of agencies, some of crucial importance, and scores of personal assistants who help the President. We talk about the "office" not the man.

Side by side with the personal element of political leadership, and often at odds with it, is the "organizational" aspect of the office. A President or a Prime Minister, especially if he is not a strong leader, may well become overshadowed by the office and fail to give to it the drive and momentum it needs. Thousands of subordinates, committees, and staff agencies may provide the knowledge and information and carry out the routine operations. Routinization of leadership leads to weak government and stalemate.

But so much for some of the developed political societies. Overriding all discussion of political forms is the question of social configuration and ideology. Social configuration involves a host of questions—population, geography, national income, per capita income, patterns of transportation and communication patterns, literacy, degree of education, diffusion of skills, and mobility from one social class to another.

Ideology is more difficult to define—it is both the way people look at the world and each other and the attitudes they share about their own system of government. Whenever people share common beliefs and accept common symbols, the system is a stable one. The reverse situation creates internal conflicts, accounts for instability, and leads to revolution.

Aristotle was the first to emphasize the importance of social structures. He singled out social classes and property, and concluded that, where property was shared by many, the result was a large middle class with similar interests and expectations. Such a system was less prone to internal conflicts. Democracy worked well because the people were so much alike in interest and status. An American sociologist, writing in a recent book called *Political Man,* has come to similar conclusions on the basis of careful study of many political societies. He has concluded that where the per capita income is the highest, where literacy is widespread, where access to education and the acquisition of skills is open and free, where the middle class is large, there democracy thrives and stability is the rule. Countries like England, Scandinavia, Switzerland, and the United States rank high in this correlation between prosperity and democracy and stability.

The correlation is exactly the reverse in some Latin American nations, Southeast Asian governments, and new African republics. We find lack of prosperity, lack of a large, homogeneous middle class, and lack of skills and opportunities correlated with instability, violence, revolution, and authoritarian and totalitarian movements. The one-party totalitarian system or the young one-party republics of North Africa, Africa, or India cannot afford the niceties of democracy or, when they try to introduce it, find that it cannot work. Conflict is born in the interstices of their socioeconomic structure. Pent-up demands and needs that cannot be easily channeled and met through the political system explode in the face of the system and revolution alternates with repressive measures. The modicum of well-being in democracies breeds tolerance. Disagreements are met by compromises rather than violence. This is not the case in most of the new nations.

Socioeconomic factors, however, are not enough to explain the disparities between democratic and non-democratic societies and to account for stability or lack of it. Basic to the fate of political societies is the manner in which people view their society and the world, that is, ideology. Ideology shapes action and attitudes; it molds the political leadership before they in turn attempt to shape the opinions of the people. Today, more than ever, the role of ideas becomes clear when we study the relatively small group of people, the political leaders and the intellectuals, who have inspired the new nations and have given meaning and content to pent-up aspirations in a world that outside of the United States, western Europe, the Scandinavian countries, and some members of the Commonwealth is a world in ferment— a ferment, by the way, from which even the Soviet leaders begin to dissociate themselves. Ideas have given a form to the previous discontent that was caused by centuries of colonial rule, misery, and degradation. They are national independence, the search for national identity, the elimination of privilege, and economic well-being and equality.

But the way in which these goals will be realized depends very much on the political ideologies of the leaders. Some leaders will believe that the way to accomplish these goals quickly is by following the Soviet model of revolution, industrialization, and one-party control. Others hesitate between the urgency to which they are committed for the accomplishments of their goals and the sacrifices that their speedy realization will entail. One-party authoritarian or totalitarian systems appear to be efficient in the short run. They mobilize the masses, eliminate privileges, and restructure the society. But they also necessitate a political control that may well outlive what some consider to be a historical necessity.

Totalitarianism is one avenue to speedy modernization. The democratic model which emphasizes individual rights, freedom of choice, and responsibility makes undue concessions to privileged groups. Such a model also is slow, and it allows for differences to lead to inaction. Some political leaders remain faithful to the goals of freedom and democracy. It is hard to expect that democracy will be accepted in countries where poverty and illiteracy are the rule. But it is not too optimistic to expect that where the process of modernization is coupled with a firm commitment to maintain freedom and choice, democracy may survive. Mexico and India, for instance, illustrate that this may well be the case. As new socioeconomic groups develop side by side with economic and social modernization, their ideas are shaped by the rule of free expression and compromise. Conflict is resolved through the existing channels of the political system. In such societies the building of a political community goes hand in hand with the acceptance of democratic ideals; democracy becomes a stable instrument of government.

17 INTERNATIONAL RELATIONS

Hans J. Morgenthau

International relations are as old as political history itself and throughout the ages they have shown constant patterns of relationships and policies, regardless of whether hereditary monarchs or elective governments, city- or nation-states, continental empires or tiny principalities, ecclesiastic or secular rulers entered into them. The consistency of patterns, beneath the variety of historic manifestations, makes both historic understanding and theoretical analysis possible. Thus we are able to understand the international relations of the Greek city-states which Thucydides describes, the international relations of the Indian states of the fourth century B.C., from which Kautilya derived his philosophy, the international relations of the ancient Near East of which the Old Testament tells, as well as those of the more recent past. By detecting in the international relations of different cultures and historic periods identical responses to identical challenges, we are able to develop certain theoretical propositions about international relations which are true regardless of time and place.

The dynamic forces that mold international relations are the aspirations for power of autonomous political units. These aspirations crystallize into three basic patterns: to keep one's power, to increase one's power, to demonstrate one's power. From these patterns three basic policies ensue: the policies of the status quo, of imperialism, and of prestige. The clash of these policies— A trying to maintain the status quo, B trying to change it at the expense of A—leads to an unending struggle for power which characterizes all international relations. This struggle for power can be fought by two different means: the peaceful means of diplomacy or military force. It leads, of necessity, to the configuration of the balance of power through which nation A, either alone or in conjunction with other nations similarly threatened, tries to maintain itself against B. Insofar as A and B pursue their goals in conjunction with other nations, they embark on a policy of alliances. Insofar as they fight the struggle for power by military means, they engage in a competition for armaments—that is, an armaments race. Insofar as they try to justify and rationalize their position in the power struggle by reference to universal values, typically of a moral nature, they develop political ideologies. Continual peaceful contacts among them lead to the development of an institutionalized diplomacy.

Throughout the better part of history, several systems of international relations have existed side by side with either intermittent or no contact with each other. Until the discovery of America, the American system or systems of international relations led a completely separate existence; their very existence was unknown to the rest of the world. The Chinese and Indian systems had only intermittent contacts with others. Three different patterns of international relations can be distinguished according to the distribution of power within them: multiple, bipolar, and imperial systems. The multiple system is distinguished by a number of units of approximately equal strength which combine and oppose each other in ever-changing alignments. Its main characteristics are flexibility, uncertainty as to the relative strength and future policies of its members, and the propensity for limited, inconclusive wars. The European state system, from the end of the Thirty Years' War in 1648 to the beginning of the First World War in 1914, with the exception of the Napoleonic Wars, conforms to this pattern.

The bipolar system is characterized by the predominance of two major powers of approximately equal strength; the other members are grouped around them in differing degrees of closeness. This system is exceptionally rigid and stable as long as the approximately equal distribution of power between its two predominant members persists. Any marked shift in that distribution threatens the system with destruction. The structure of international relations that emerged from the Second World War exemplifies this pattern.

The imperial system consists of one predominant member and a number of subordinate members clustered around it. Its stability is great, and conflicts within it tend to be marginal. The system's existence can be threatened by the disintegration of the predominant member, by the rise of a number of subordinate members to a position from which they can challenge the predominant one, and by a challenge from outside the system. The system of international relations dominated by the Roman Empire is the classic example of this pattern.

International relations have undergone four drastic changes in modern times: the formerly separate systems of international relations have merged into one world-wide system; the predominance of the European system has disappeared; the possibility and actuality of total war dominate the international scene; the feasibility of universal destruction with nuclear weapons has radically altered the function of force as a means to the ends of foreign policy. The first three changes do not affect the dynamics and structure of international relations as we have known them since the beginning of political history, but the last change constitutes a veritable revolution, the only one in recorded history, in the structure of international relations.

The expansion of the European state system into the other continents by means of colonial empires, from the beginning of the sixteenth to the end of the nineteenth century, broke down the barrier that had separated the different systems of international relations. They were all brought into contact with, and into some form of dependence upon, the European state system, and through it they came into contact with each other. The two world wars of this century, in which most nations of the world participated, point in their very name to the transformation of a number of separate systems of international relations into one worldwide system. That process of political unification was greatly advanced and expanded to the individual sphere through the development of the technology of transportation and communications. This development started with the great voyage at the end of the fifteenth century and culminated in our time in the drastic reduction of geographic distances for transportation and the virtual obliteration of the limits of time and space for communications.

The last phase of this transformation of international relations into a worldwide system, covering roughly the period from the end of the First World War to the aftermath of the Second, coincides with a radical change in the distribution of power within the system. From the beginning of the sixteenth century to the First World War the European system provided the dynamics and the preponderant power for this transformation; today, two either completely or predominantly non-European nations, the United States and the Soviet Union, have taken its place. This decline of Europe as the political center of the world can be said to have started with the Monroe Doctrine of 1823 declaring the mutual political independence of Europe and the Western Hemisphere. This declaration of political emancipation on behalf of former colonies of European nations foreshadowed the fragmentation of the European empires which was virtually consummated after the Second World War in the form of colonial revolution sweeping Africa and Asia. Most of the European colonial possessions, one after the other, have gained their national independence, and many of them have either withdrawn their political support from the European nations or joined their enemies. The outstanding examples of these two different forms of political emancipation are India and China, respectively.

The decline of Europe as a result of the colonial revolutions coincides with the rise to predominance of formerly backward nations, such as Russia and China. This is the result of the technological unification of the world that has given these nations the tools with which to transform their superior potential in geography, population, and natural resources into the actuality of national power.

The two world wars of this century are the decisive factor in the decline of Europe as the political center of the world. At the same time as they weakened the main European nations in their human and material resources, they brought non-European nations to the fore, the United States and Japan after the First World War, the United States and the Soviet Union after the Second. These two world wars differ not only in their consequences but also in their intrinsic character from the wars that have been fought in the Western world in modern times. Most previous wars were limited: only a fraction of the total human and material resources of the belligerents was committed to the war, only a fraction of the total population was morally identified with the war and suffered from it, and the war was waged only for limited objectives. The two world wars and those for which the most powerful nations prepare today are total in all these respects. The actuality and threat of total war are indeed the most important distinctive characteristics of contemporary international relations. This threat of war is caused by an unprecedented accumulation of destructive power in the hands of the most powerful nations and the incentive to use that power for national purposes. The accumulation of power results from drastic changes in the distribution of political and technological power in the world; the incentive is presented by the closing of the colonial frontier and the ascendancy of a universalistic nationalism.

Throughout the modern period, with the exception of the religious wars of the sixteenth and seventeenth centuries and the Napoleonic Wars, wars were limited in every respect. Power was so widely dispersed among a great number of sovereign states that no single state or possible combination of them was strong enough to gain more than limited objectives against its adversaries. The drastic numerical reduction of sovereign states and the resulting concentration of power in the hands of a few nations of the first rank, which occurred between the end of the Thirty Years' War and the end of the Second World War, created one precondition for total war. The Treaty of Westphalia of 1648, for instance, reduced the number of sovereign states of which the German Empire was composed from 900 to 355. The Diet of Regensburg of 1803 eliminated 200 more. When the German Confederation was founded in 1815, only 36 sovereign states were left to join it. The unification of Italy in 1859 and that of Germany in 1871 eliminated 31 additional sovereign states.

At the end of the Napoleonic Wars in 1815, only five nations of the first rank were left—Austria, France, Great Britain, Russia, and Prussia. In the sixties, Italy and the United States joined them, followed toward the end of the century by Japan. At the beginning of the First World War in 1914, eight nations were of the first rank, with Germany having replaced Prussia. Since the end of the First World War, the trend toward reduction of the number of sovereign states has been reversed and their number has about doubled because of the successive breakup of the Ottoman, Austrian-Hungarian, British, and French Empires. Yet the trend toward the concentration of more and more power in the hands of fewer and fewer states has continued and at the end of the Second World War the number of nations of the first rank was reduced to two—the United States and the Soviet Union.

It is not by accident that the two most powerful nations, capable of threatening each other with total war, are also the most advanced technologically and industrially. For the mechanization of warfare in terms of weapons, supplies, transportation, and communications, requires, in case of actual hostilities, the virtually total commitment of the industrial productivity of the nation. This total commitment has been made possible by the enormous increase in economic productivity brought about by a series of technological and industrial revolutions, starting in the eighteenth century. By contrast, in previous periods of history, economic productivity was so low that after it had barely provided for the necessities

of life of the population, little was left for military purposes. Thus premodern technology could support only
limited war, whereas modern industry is productive
enough to allow the commitment of the lion's share of
its products for military purposes.

One incentive for the great nations to use this enormous productive power for the purposes of mutual destruction has been provided by a change in international
relations which can be called the disappearance of the
colonial frontier. The generally limited character of the
means and ends of foreign policy from the end of the
Middle Ages to the First World War was in good measure due to the opportunity for the great European nations to seek satisfaction for their power aspirations not
in all-out contest with each other but through competitive expansion into three continents—Africa, the Ameri-
cas, and the part of Asia bordering on the Eastern oceans.
Colonial competition and conflict during that period
were main outlets through which the European nations
could compete for power without endangering their
existence. At the beginning of the twentieth century,
the colonial frontier was, for all practical purposes,
closed—virtually all politically weak or empty spaces
around the globe had been transformed into colonies or
spheres of influence by one of the European nations.
From then on, as the two world wars show, the great
European powers, deprived of the colonial safety valve,
fought each other not for limited advantage but for total
stakes, and they could do so with the instruments of total
war.

These stakes have become total not only because total
war threatens the belligerents with total destruction but
also because the issue over which nations compete and
fight has become total. That issue is no longer a limited
military or territorial advantage but the universal tri-

umph or defeat of a particular philosophy and a way of life, which are supposed to be incarnate in a particular nation. Whereas traditionally the international relations of the Western world were carried on within the framework of common moral principles and a common way of life, which imposed effective limitations upon the struggle for power, in our age international relations are dominated by the conflict between democracy and communism, each putting forth a message of universal salvation, each trying—with differing intensity—to extend its dominion to all mankind, and each identified with one of the two great powers left in the world. Thus international relations today are characterized not only by the traditional threat and use of military force on behalf of the aspirations of individual nations but also by a struggle for the minds of men through which the proponents of the two antagonistic philosophies and ways of life—using the instruments of propaganda, foreign aid, and foreign trade—endeavor to gain the allegiance of uncommitted nations. By the same token, the traditional methods of diplomacy are in eclipse; although nations can negotiate and bargain about their interests and conclude compromises concerning them, they feel that they cannot yield an inch where their philosophies and ways of life are at stake.

Similar situations have existed before, temporarily and on a limited scale, especially in periods of religious conflicts and wars, but present-day international relations are marked by a change in structure unprecedented in recorded history. Throughout history there has existed a rational relationship between the threat and use of military force and the ends of foreign policy. It was rational for a nation to ask itself whether it could achieve its ends vis-à-vis another nation by peaceful means or whether it had to resort to military force in order to achieve them. For the risks involved in the resort to military force were generally not out of proportion to the ends sought. Great ends justified great risks, since the risks were generally not so great as to obviate the ends. Yet all-out nuclear war, likely to destroy all belligerents and thus eliminate the very distinction between victor and vanquished, is a completely irrational undertaking. Because no possible end is able to justify it, it is an instrument of mass murder and mass suicide.

Contemporary international relations are faced with two interconnected dilemmas; on the solution to these dilemmas depends the survival certainly of Western civilization and perhaps of mankind itself. The first dilemma consists in the contrast between the technological unification of the world and the parochial moral commitments and political institutions of the age. Moral commitments and political institutions, dating from an age which modern technology has left behind, have not kept pace with technological achievements and, hence, are incapable of controlling their destructive potentialities. The second dilemma consists in the contrast between the need of nations to support their interests by resort to violence and the irrationality of resort to nuclear arms. If a nation cannot resort to nuclear weapons without risking its own destruction, how can it support its interests in a world of sovereign nations which is ruled by violence as the last resort?

Five main answers have been given to this question: disarmament, collective security, international government, the world state, and diplomacy. It must be noted that most attempts at securing international peace through disarmament have failed and the two that succeeded, the Rush-Bagot Agreement of 1817 demilitarizing the American-Canadian frontier and the

Washington Treaty for the Limitation of Naval Armaments of 1922, were an integral part of a political settlement that carried in itself the assurance of peace. In other words, as the armaments race is a symptom of political conflict which is likely to lead to war, so is disarmament the symptom of the disappearance of political tension which by itself gives assurance for the preservation of peace.

Collective security assumes that nations generally increase their armaments and go to war either because they are in fear of aggression or because they trust that aggression will succeed without too great a risk. If the community of nations could provide its members with security through collective action, the main motive for war would then disappear. In a system of collective security, security is the concern of all nations which will take care collectively of the security of each of them as though their own security were at stake. If nation *A* threatens nation *B*'s security, *C, D, E, F, G* will take measures on behalf of *B* and against *A* as though *A* threatened them, and vice versa.

The ability of a system of collective security to preserve peace rests on three assumptions: (1) The collective system must have at its disposal at all times sufficient strength to deter any potential aggressor. (2) The nations which dispose of such overwhelming strength must have the same interest in defending the status quo. (3) These nations must subordinate their conflicting political interests to the overriding concern for collective defense. The history of collective security shows that these three conditions are rarely present at the same time. First of all, history shows that aggression is generally threatened or committed not by one but several nations which, at least initially, are of approximately equal if not superior strength to those who are willing to resist aggression.

The reason for this state of affairs must be sought in the fact that what is required for the security of one group of nations may be incompatible with, or actually threaten the security of, another group of nations. Finally, collective security presupposes a moral transformation which makes individual nations forego their national egotisms and the national policies serving them for the sake of collective policies serving the supranational objective.

International government is different from the devices to establish international peace discussed thus far in that the latter intend to provide specific remedies for a particular problem, while international government recognizes that peace and order can be secure only in an integrated society, existing under a common authority and a common conception of justice. International government, then, is the attempt to establish such an authority and to create such a conception of justice in a society of sovereign states.

The United Nations was conceived as international government of the great powers; this is obvious from the membership and the functions of the Security Council. The ability of such an international organization to protect the peace of the world, then, depends on the ability of the great powers to work in unison for the achievement of that objective. Yet thus far the particular interests of individual great powers have tended by and large to prevail over the interest that they were supposed to have in common: the preservation of peace.

The United Nations has as its basic political objective the maintenance of the status quo as it had been established at the end of the Second World War. However, not all the great nations had the same understanding as to what the maintenance of the status quo meant in view of their particular interests, nor were all of them equally interested in the maintenance of that status quo. Thus it came about that the United Nations has been paralyzed from the very beginning as a peacemaker by the conflict between the Western world and the Soviet bloc.

The attempts to secure peace by an international government of sovereign nations have all been the victim of a contradiction inherent in these very attempts. The establishment of effective government over sovereign nations seems to be a contradiction in terms which can be eliminated only by a direct attack on national sovereignty itself.

The world state, then, seems to offer a logical solution to the problem of international peace. In the same way, so it is argued, in which domestic peace has been made secure by the subjection of local and regional governments to a common authority, so international peace, to be secure, must be built on the foundations of a government for all mankind to which national governments must yield their sovereignty.

Any world government, if it is not to be tyrannical, must rest on a triple foundation: supranational loyalties, common expectations of justice, and overwhelming power. That is to say, whenever a conflict arises between loyalty to a particular nation and loyalty to the world government, the latter must be reasonably certain that the conflict will be resolved in its favor. Furthermore, the peoples of the world must be united in the reasonable expectation that the world government will at least approximate justice in its dealings with them. Finally, the world government must have at its disposal such overwhelming physical strength as will make unlikely from the outset physical resistance to its decisions on the part of any group subject to its rule.

Diplomacy, however, has remained the chief instrumentality through which states have actually attempted to preserve international peace by reconciling hostile interests that threaten to lead to war. Diplomacy is the oldest and, as it were, the most natural method for the settlement of international disputes; for sovereign entities, such as nations, which by definition are not subject to a higher authority, must naturally try to settle their disputes peacefully by way of negotiations—that is, through diplomacy. The decisive factor in such diplomatic negotiations is the interest of the negotiating parties in the success of the negotiations. This interest generally takes two different forms. On the one hand, the negotiating parties expect from the peaceful settlement the protection and promotion of their vital interests, while both are willing to compromise on secondary issues, thus each giving up something and receiving something. On the other hand, the interest of the parties in concluding an agreement and, more particularly, in keeping it depends upon the political and military pressures which one side is able to exert upon the other in support of a peaceful settlement. This has been one of the traditional functions of competitive armaments, alliances, and the balance of power.

Diplomacy as a method of preserving peace has in the past been deprecated in the measure in which the newer methods have captured the popular imagination. That deprecation is based on moral as well as practical grounds. Whereas diplomacy is defective on both counts, governments, while experimenting with the newer methods, have continued to rely mainly upon the traditional methods of diplomacy. It is worthy of note to what extent, for instance, the United Nations, which was supposed to provide a substitute for the traditional methods of diplomacy, has been transformed into an instrument of diplomacy, used by individual nations for the protection and promotion of their particular interests.

However, the search for a more effective method of preserving peace than diplomacy can provide—a search that has occupied humanity to an ever-increasing extent since the beginning of the nineteenth century—reflects the new and ever-increasing urgency that the problem of peace has taken on in our time. The political, technological, and moral revolutions of our time have transformed war from the rational instrument of foreign policy which it once was into an instrument of universal destruction. It is one of the great paradoxes of our age that the preservation of peace has become a matter of survival for Western civilization, while the traditional instruments of preserving it have become less effective and more effective ones have not yet been devised.

Grateful acknowledgment is made to the *Encyclopaedia Britannica*, from which this chapter has been adapted.

18 UNITED STATES FOREIGN POLICY AND THE UNITED NATIONS

Gerard J. Mangone

AMERICAN SUPPORT OF THE UNITED NATIONS

In July 1945, just before the guns of World War II were silenced, the Senate of the United States, by a vote of 89 in favor and 2 opposed, approved the ratification of the Charter of the United Nations. Since then, for almost twenty years, Americans have overwhelmingly endorsed the idea of a permanent international organization designed to maintain international peace and to develop friendly relations among nations based on respect for self-determination, equal rights, and economic cooperation.

Today virtually all modern states conduct their foreign policies through bilateral arrangements, and through regional agreements with several other states, as well as in the councils of the United Nations with its specialized and affiliated agencies. Among the leading powers of the world none has given greater support to the United Nations than the United States, for, as President Lyndon Johnson observed in his address before the Eighteenth Session of the General Assembly, "We support the United Nations as the best instrument yet devised to promote the peace of the world and the well-being of mankind."

In 1946 the United Nations received $8.5 million from an American citizen, Mr. John D. Rockefeller, Jr., to pay for the land that the United Nations now uses for its headquarters in New York. Two years later the United States government lent the United Nations $65 million in order to construct its buildings, a loan that is repayable over a period of thirty-one years with no interest charges to the United Nations. In fact, between 1946 and 1963, Americans have contributed through their taxes over $2 billion to the United Nations system.

Jet-propelled transportation and electronics communication facilities are drawing the states of the world even closer to each other. Their economic life increasingly depends upon sound international trade, better labor standards, and generous financial cooperation; conditions of health and social justice, moreover, can no longer be hidden behind frontiers; and international war has become such a devastating horror, threatening every man, woman, and child with its terrible power, that all governments must be concerned about maintaining worldwide peace.

The United States has never regarded the United Nations as a world government. Americans believe in the ideals of national self-determination, as set forth by President Woodrow Wilson in 1917, when, speaking before the Senate of the United States, he said, "no nation should seek to extend its polity over any other nation or people, but every people should be left free to determine its own polity, its own way of development, unhindered, unthreatened, unafraid, the little along with the great and powerful." The United Nations, however, is an organization through which the opinion of mankind can be heard and by which effective international remedies can be devised to prevent the outbreaks of violence throughout the world. It is, moreover, an agency through which multinational cooperative effort can preserve international peace by raising economic levels, by improving social standards, and by strengthening legal norms in every country of the world.

PEACE-KEEPING

For five years after its founding, the United Nations had shown little or no strength—other than passing resolutions and sending investigatory missions—in carrying out its mandate to maintain peace. The Security Council seemed ineffectual in its efforts to deal with violence in Palestine, Indonesia, Greece, and Kashmir. In 1950, however, the United States boldly took the lead in supporting the first collective security action of the United Nations as it repelled the aggression by North Korea against South Korea.

Fifty-three members of the United Nations endorsed the principle of collective security in Korea, while fifteen nations, other than the United States, actually offered ground, naval, or air forces to be placed under United Nations command. To be sure, 90 per cent of the non-Korean forces in the field were American, but the attack upon South Korea, recognized in 1948 by the General Assembly as a lawful government, was a direct attack upon the United Nations itself. Only the resolute action of the Security Council in condemning this aggression and the swift support of South Korea furnished by the United States proved to the world that the United Nations could play a vital role in deterring aggression. If the United Nations had failed to act in Korea, it might well have lost the faith of all its members and thereafter remained only a hollow-sounding conference hall, powerless to act in the cause of peace.

In 1956 the United States once again joined virtually

all members of the United Nations in a ringing denunciation of the aggression against Egypt committed by the United Kingdom, France, and Israel. The American people acted with no malice against old friends and they held no special affection for the regime in Cairo. But the President and Congress earnestly believed that the unprovoked attack of any one state by another, anywhere in the world, must be investigated and stopped in accordance with the United Nations Charter. Only then could all governments cooperate in healing the wounds of discord through international economic assistance and dispassionate legal judgments. To preserve that uneasy peace between Israel and Egypt in the Gaza Strip, the United States between 1956 and 1962 willingly contributed over $57 million to the United Nations Emergency Force or approximately 44 per cent of its total cost.

The third major peace-keeping effort of the UN supported by the people of the United States has been in the troubled Congo. On July 12, 1960, the President and the Prime Minister of the Congo cabled the Secretary General of the United Nations requesting the "urgent dispatch by the United Nations of military assistance." The Congolese government justified its request by condemning the unsolicited intervention of Belgium to restore order in the area and protect Europeans, calling the intervention "an act of aggression." Two days later, even though Britain, France, and China abstained, the United States voted in favor of Tunisia's resolution in the Security Council that called, first, for the withdrawal of Belgian troops from the territory of the Congo and, second, authorized the Secretary General to provide the government of the Congo with such military assistance as may be necessary to enable the national security forces "to meet fully their tasks."

The action of the United Nations in the Congo has not been without its critics. As Secretary General U Thant has said, "Quite possibly no activity ever engaged in by the United Nations has suffered so much as the Congo operation from public misunderstanding of its purposes and activities." The support of the legal but politically divided government by the United Nations police force only a few weeks after the Congo's independence obviously influenced the internal affairs of the country. Yet Belgium did withdraw its troops and public order was generally restored. Even though internal Congolese strife could not be solved by the multinational battalions of the United Nations, foreign intervention by any single state was definitely prevented by international action.

From July 1960 through December 1962 the total expenses for the UN operation in the Congo ran to approximately $300 million, of which the United States paid $73.5 million as part of its assessment under the Charter and voluntarily contributed another $40.9 million to military and economic needs. Or, put another way, the American people paid for 38 per cent of the costs of the international engagement in the Congo designed to prevent aggression and to maintain public order.

Because certain states of the United Nations refused to pay their assessments for the costs of the Middle East and Congo peace-keeping activities, the international organization found itself financially embarrassed. Early in 1964 the United Nations was in debt for $134 million. The International Court of Justice had solemnly advised the United Nations in 1962 that the expenditures authorized by both Security Council and General Assembly peace-keeping resolutions on the Middle East and the Congo constituted expenses of the organization within the meaning of Article 17, Paragraph 2, of the Charter; that is, they were expenses that ought to be borne by members of the organization as apportioned by the General Assembly. The United States has strongly supported that legal position. A United Nations police force, like the police force of any community, serves the interest of all its members in maintaining order. The United States believes that the expenses of the organization should be provided by all members according to their ability to pay and the general apportionment of expenses made by the General Assembly pursuant to the Charter.

Not all the disputes between states have been settled in the United Nations. Every serious statesman recognizes that the world is still a dangerous place of contending national interests that somehow must be peacefully accommodated. In some instances, such as in Hungary and Goa, the international organization has been powerless to act. On November 4, 1956, for example, the United States presented a draft resolution to the Security Council calling on the Soviet Union "to desist forthwith from any form of intervention, particularly armed intervention in the internal affairs of Hungary . . . and to cease the introduction of additional armed forces into Hungary." Nine members of the Security Council voted in favor of this resolution, with only the Soviet Union opposed and thereby vetoing the resolution. Five days later the General Assembly approved a resolution strongly supported by the United States calling on the Soviet Union to withdraw its troops without further delay and asking the Secretary General to investigate the situation. But the revolutionary government of Hungary had already been overthrown by Russian military might and the new government absolutely forbade any investigation by the United Nations.

Even though deeply committed to Indian economic development, and most friendly to the Indian people, the United States could not accept the military take-over of Portuguese Goa by India on December 18, 1961, as consonant with the ideals of the United Nations Charter. The United States joined six other members in the Security Council in calling for a cease fire and the withdrawal of Indian forces from the territory—all to no avail, for the Soviet Union vetoed the resolution.

Once again a principle was involved: the obligation to settle international disputes by peaceful means and to refrain from the threat of use of force in international disputes. Force can be permitted only when used in actual individual or collective self-defense or when sanctioned by the authority of the United Nations Charter itself. In its foreign policy, the United States has adhered to this principle—whether in Yemen, Cuba, Malaysia, or Cyprus—so that it can assist the United Nations in its primary function; namely, the maintenance of international peace and security.

ECONOMIC AND SOCIAL ACTIVITIES

Major support for the economic and social activities of the United Nations and its affiliated agencies has also been advanced by the United States. For example, between 1946 and 1963 the American people contributed about $300 million to the Expanded Fund for Technical Assistance and the Special Fund, another $300 million for the UN Relief and Works Agency for Palestine Refugees, and $250 million for the International Refugee Organization. Almost a quarter of a billion dollars has been donated by America for the UN International Children's Emergency Fund during the last fourteen years, more than all the contributions of all the other states of the world put together.

The larger share of United States foreign economic assistance, of course, is carried out through bilateral agreements between the United States and recipient countries, for Americans, like other peoples of the world, want some direct control over their tax expenditures both at home and abroad. The administrative problems of many multilateral organizations, moreover, sometimes do not permit flexible programs of economic assistance that may be most desirable for a particular country. These can often be accomplished more speedily and efficiently by a bilateral arrangement with the United States.

There are many advantages to UN-sponsored economic and social programs. Such international programs involve the effort and, therefore, the responsibility of the community of nations; they call upon a multiplicity of national talents and may rouse less resentment among developing nations who suspect the foreign policy of any one state. The challenge to American statesmen, therefore, has been to combine an imaginative program of bilateral loans and grants to selected countries for selected purposes with a continually increasing support of UN economic and social activities.

From the end of World War II through 1962, the United States granted approximately $40.2 billion (net) in economic and technical assistance to other states of the world. It also made available about $20.5 billion to foreign nations in credits and loans, over half of which has been collected, but often in currency not convertible into dollars. Finally, the United States has given economic assistance to peoples in other countries by selling some $8 billion of American farm products for local currencies, generally not convertible into dollars.

Whereas the funds appropriated for the United Nations and other international organizations under United States foreign assistance acts have been comparatively small, ordinarily used for technical assistance, refugee relief, and so forth, the funds appropriated to the President for international use have been considerably larger. In fiscal year 1963, for example, $60 million was appropriated by the Congress for the Inter-American Bank, $61.6 million for a subscription to the International Development Association, and $2 billion for a loan to the International Monetary Fund. Moreover, the United States has subscribed $635 million to the capital of the International Bank for Reconstruction and Development. To sum up, between 1945 and 1963, the United States invested over $5 billion in the Inter-American Development Bank and the four major international finance institutions that have been established under the UN system.

In addition to the United Nations, with its nine specialized agencies, its international financial agencies, and its several voluntary programs, the United States participates in the work of no fewer than twenty-four other public international organizations, ranging from the International Bureau of Weights and Measures to the International Atomic Energy Agency. Regional problems, moreover, are frequently channeled through the Organization of American States, the South Pacific Commission, or the Organization for Economic Cooperation and Development in Europe. This complex international network of political, economic, or social agencies tremendously assists the United States in adjusting its national policies peacefully to a reasonable accommodation with the needs and aspirations of other states, thus creating a community of world interests, which is the best safeguard of international law.

247

FORMULATING POLICY THROUGH INTERNATIONAL ORGANIZATIONS

The Department of State of the United States is primarily responsible for the conduct of American foreign policy, whether in bilateral negotiations, regional arrangements, or through the United Nations system. The State Department was the first executive department created under the Constitution of 1789, and it holds a special place in American government. Above all, the State Department advises the President and, by his direction, informs the Congress about foreign affairs, presenting recommendations to both branches of American government so that they may in concert judiciously exercise their constitutional authority to make foreign policy by executive orders or the enactment of appropriate legislation.

The Bureau of International Organization Affairs, headed by an Assistant Secretary of State, provides the necessary guidance and support for United States participation in international organizations and conferences, and it prepares United States positions on international organization matters. In addition to the two deputies and the four special assistants or advisers to the Assistant Secretary, the Bureau comprises an office of UN political affairs, an office of international economic and social affairs, an office of international administration, and an office of international conferences. In 1963 the Bureau was manned by a staff of approximately 170 people.

The United States, like other members of the United Nations, also maintains a mission in New York. The United States Representative to the United Nations, as well as its Representative in the Security Council, is

Adlai E. Stevenson, twice a candidate for the Presidency of the United States, and one of the most distinguished citizens of America. Despite its responsibilities, the United States Mission to the United Nations comprises a relatively small staff of 120 people, of whom about one-third are professional. These men and women conduct the day-to-day negotiations of American foreign policy in the councils and committees of the United Nations, acting upon information and advice from the Bureau of International Organization Affairs and directions from the President or the Secretary of State.

The coordination of modern foreign policy, which must today take into account military, economic, and ideological interests that overflow frontiers with dazzling rapidity, troubles all statesmen. The United States, with its enormous resources and its sense of responsibility for peaceful change, has endeavored to utilize the means of foreign policy that most efficiently and most appropriately accomplish the aims of the American people; namely, international security, improved economic standards, and human freedom. Bilateral alliances, regional security pacts, like the North Atlantic Treaty Organization, and peace-keeping through the United Nations have all been combined to deter aggression. Economic and technical aid programs have been fostered through the American foreign assistance acts, through support of the regional Organization of American States, and through the expanded program of Technical Assistance and the Special Fund of the United Nations. All these programs have been supported simultaneously by the United States in order to gain flexibility and efficiency in foreign policy by applying American resources to either bilateral or multilateral agreements as both national and international needs may require.

International organizations represent a relatively new

and rapidly widening avenue for the traffic of diplomacy. In a single month some forty or fifty councils, commissions, or main committees meet under the auspices of the United Nations system alone. In shaping its foreign policies, the United States increasingly enters the world forum that has been provided by international organizations, for there the peoples of the world can be rallied to support collective action to maintain peace, to stimulate the economies of underdeveloped countries, or to ensure that human rights are not abridged or denied anywhere.

Bilateral and regional arrangements between states, of course, will and should continue, but the evidence of history and the hopes for the future seem to point to an ever-expanding role for international organizations within the family of the United Nations. As Secretary of State Dean Rusk has boldly stated, "While nations may cling to national values and ideas and ambitions and prerogatives, science has created a functional international society, whether we like it or not."

The United Nations began its stormy life after a terrible period of two world wars, widespread poverty, and a failure to realize the brotherhood and dignity of man that all great religions preach. From 51 nations it has grown to 114; its administrative and programmatic budgets have multiplied several times; and its involvement in international affairs everywhere in the world has quickened to a degree never anticipated by its founders. The foreign policy of the United States continues to be steadfastly committed to this robust development of peace by international accommodation and economic advance by multilateral cooperation, always pushing forward the frontiers of civilization by an international law that will nourish the improved standards of human rights.

19 SCIENCE AND GOVERNMENT

Avery Leiserson

I shall try to view the effects of science on the agenda
and institutions of government in the United States
against the background of certain universal trends in the
position and functioning of science in modern civilization.[1]

The first kind of universal trend I want to identify
concerns the relation between "science and the citizen."
In the popular view, science has acquired tremendous
prestige. People attribute to scientists the power, for
both good and evil, to provide the essential weapons of
national defense and space exploration; to wrest from
nature its ultimate secrets (the convertibility of matter
and energy, the relativity of time and space); to understand the origins and to control the environment of
human life, disease and health, even to create the industrial and economic conditions under which poverty
and unemployment can effectively be abolished. This
"cult" of science helps to undermine the outmoded view
based on authority and superstition. Throughout the
world people today accept the pragmatic testing of scientific hypotheses in personal medicine and health,
farming and food production, industrial processes and

1 See Thorstein Veblen, "The Place of Science in Modern Civilization,"
American Journal of Sociology, XI (1906), 1–31.

products which only a generation or two ago ran counter to the most deep-seated ethical, religious, and social convictions.

Not only in the academic environment of universities, but also in industry, government, professional societies, and voluntary groups of all kinds, the desirability of research is coming to be accepted as a condition of growth and success in achieving the purposes of enterprise. Taxpayers have been consenting for years to the appropriation of billions of dollars for public education for their children as a means to personal success in life. Nowadays they accept the necessity of investing millions more for organized research—the expansion of scientific knowledge—as a condition for the advancement and survival of society itself.[2]

There is almost universal recognition of the need for all children to have a minimum training in science in order to know how to behave as citizens in modern urbanized communities, to understand, for example, the elementary rules of sanitation and safety in ordinary living—the pollution of water, air, food; the uses of fire, gas, or electricity; to say nothing of the more complex problems of air and auto transportation, population growth, and international trade.

Such ideas as these, widely and popularly held, have produced great changes in the scientific community. No longer do scientists think of themselves as isolated laboratory workers. They recognize the importance of government support of their research requiring expensive equipment, facilities, and personnel support, vastly exceeding the scale that, historically speaking, private donors and industrial interests were able to

2 F. Machlup, *The Production and Distribution of Knowledge in the United States* (Princeton, N.J.: Princeton University Press, 1962), chap. 5.

provide. The *interdependence* of science and government, science and industry, and science and technology has become a byword. Scientists have become aware of their social responsibility for the destructive as well as the beneficent uses of their ideas and instruments. Some of them, at least, feel compelled to make public statements about the appropriate policies governing such uses. Having accepted for the most part the consequences of government support for research, including the allocation of public funds for certain kinds of scientific research at the expense of others, scientists have reversed their historic, apolitical posture and today both seek and accept representation in the official personnel and processes of planning and financial decision-making that affect future scientific progress. The same is true in large-scale industrial organizations.

Finally, scientists have begun to realize that government support of research means that project directors have to become administrators—to plan, promote, report on, and extend their research programs. They cannot confine themselves solely to the conduct and personal supervision of laboratory operations. The conditions of scientific work are changing, and apparently scientists themselves are very much concerned, as well as at odds, about the prospects of recruiting creative research talent under modern bureaucratized conditions in contrast to the older model of the lonely genius, the self-made inventor, the thinker on his own. The world of science has been invaded by the world of politics, but the process works in reverse as well.

Perhaps the most important aspect of the relation between science and the citizen is the scientist's optimistic, everyday faith that creative intelligence can be put to work in the investigation and analysis of the human problems of civilization.[3] Science offers the revolutionary vision that the history of man and his institutions is a process of unending change; that man, by discovering the underlying processes by which he is controlled, may learn how *within limits* to modify, shape, and plan the course of his "creative evolution"; that people are capable of developing the necessary political institutions whereby they can participate in and accept the necessary restraints involved in formulating attainable goals of collective effort at given stages of development, including the consequences of bureaucratic and judicial administration for their achievement.[4]

With these universal trends as background, what can be meaningfully said about the impact of modern science upon the agenda, the everyday business of government? Here I must speak primarily of the United States. It is only recently that scholars have begun to look into the stimulating effects of scientific inquiries on the growth of governmental functions.[5] In the United States this began early in the nineteenth century. The famed Lewis and Clark expedition to the Oregon country in 1803, although it had political overtones, was also a scientific enterprise. It foreshadowed extensive use of the Army and Navy for geologic and geodetic surveys, which were subsequently turned over to civilian bureaus to provide basic data for commercial shipping and the extractive mineral industries. A legacy to the United States government from the Englishman Smithson resulted in the establishment of the famous institution that

3 D. Lerner, ed., *The Human Meaning of the Social Sciences* (Cleveland, Ohio: World Publishing Co., 1959), pp. 14–42.

4 C. E. Merriam, *Political Power* (Glencoe, Ill.: The Free Press, 1950), chap. 10; *The Role of Politics in Social Change* (New York: New York University Press, 1936), chaps. 3–4.

5 A. H. Dupree, *Science in the Federal Government* (Cambridge: Harvard University Press, 1960).

today bears his name and still carries on extensive zo-ological and anthropological inquiries. The Navy has a long tradition of astronomical observation and nonmilitary laboratory investigation in addition to its responsibilities for weapons research and polar exploration. The Weather Bureau's programs help shipping, farmers, coast dwellers, and the airlines; they are also an important part of space research. Work on weights and measures developed into the government laboratories of the National Bureau of Standards. The need for reliable information on the growth, distribution, and mobility of population, the flow of money and credit, commodity production and sales, employment, hours, wages, and conditions of work resulted in the statistical agencies of the Census Bureau, the Federal Reserve Board, the Bureaus of Labor Statistics, Agricultural Economics, and Foreign and Domestic Commerce. Perhaps the first large-scale application of scientific research to methods of farm production and management occurred shortly after the turn of the century, through cooperative arrangements between the Agricultural Research and Extension Services of the U.S. Department of Agriculture, experiment stations at the state universities, and the educational work of the county agents with individual farmers and farm organizations. Conservation of forests and timber, fish and wildlife, and oil and mineral resources, as well as land use and soil conservation began early in the present century, when such duties were authorized by law and delegated to important bureaus of the Departments of Agriculture and Interior. It was also early in the present century that government research and regulation of food processing and the production and sale of drugs was enacted over the bitter opposition of the affected industries.

This brief sketch of the growth of government services out of the need for scientific information about the natural and human environment takes no account of the application of scientific technology and automation in such government enterprises as the Post Office, Bureau of Printing and Engraving, Social Security Administration, Veterans' Administration, Federal Bureau of Investigation, the Internal Revenue Service, and other parts of the Treasury. Many of their responsibilities would be almost impossible to perform without the use of modern machine methods. In the last dozen years such techniques have resulted in the reduction of thousands of government employees in specific agencies and have contributed to a stabilized, or slightly declining, proportion of federal civilian employees to the total population—about 2.5 million out of 190 million. It is interesting to note that the 165,000 scientists and engineers employed by the federal government is about 6 per cent of all federal employment, as compared with 2.7 million, or about 1.4 per cent of the entire population.

Down to the advent of the New Deal of Franklin Roosevelt, it is fair to say that the impact of science on the agenda of American government was highly ad hoc, decentralized, the product of organized pressure aimed at achieving particular purposes at any one time. A major shift in this approach came in 1933 when the Tennessee Valley Authority was created deliberately with the multipurpose objective of river and regional development through flood control, navigation, and electric power. Scientific knowledge supported every aspect of TVA operations. Although the TVA stood by itself as a "yardstick" experiment and was not adopted for other sections of the country, it stood as a landmark demonstrating the possibilities of coordinated responsibility and imaginative planning of governmental programs. But it was not until the so-called scientific war of 1939–1945, with the spectacular advent of radar and nuclear energy, that the transformation took place in the American government's financial support and systematic attention to scientific development as a major national asset. From a total of perhaps $70 million for research and development in 1938,[6] the federal government increased these expenditures to an estimated $15 billion in 1964–1965, or from less than .1 per cent of the entire federal budget to 15 per cent. About $1.5 billion of this expenditure goes for basic scientific research, the remainder for applied uses and engineering development. What is perhaps more important is that agencies of the federal government spend only 20 per cent directly of the total research and development appropriations; almost two-thirds is spent by contract with private industry, and almost one-fifth by contract or outright grants to universities, university research centers, and nonprofit private research corporations.[7] The result is a settled pattern for achieving the expansion of knowledge as a public purpose through government financing and private performance without any major increase in the federal bureaucracy.[8]

The largest proportion of national research funds, almost one-half ($7 billion), is spent for purposes related to national security, but not all these expenditures are military in character, and in recent years they have been declining. The next largest category, almost $5 billion, or one-third of the total, is for space exploration, and $1.5 billion is spent for atomic energy research and development. The remaining $1.5 billion for research and

[6] National Resources Committee, *Research: A National Resource* (Washington, D.C.: U.S. Government Printing Office, 1938).

[7] National Science Foundation, *Annual Report* (1963); *Federal Funds for Science* (Washington, D.C.: U.S. Government Printing Office, annually).

[8] Don K. Price, *Government and Science* (New York: New York University Press, 1954).

development is spent by the Department of Health, Education and Welfare, the National Science Foundation, the Department of Agriculture, and other civilian agencies.

Any account of expenditures for scientific research and development in America would be misleading if it left the impression that American science is concerned only with national defense, space, atomic energy, and public health. A great deal of government activity, not only of a research character, goes into programs concerned with the kind and level of economic activity in both public and private sectors of the economy, from the encouragement of new inventions, materials, processes, and products to the provision of money, credit, and tax policies necessary for a steadily growing economy operating at optimum levels of production and employment. An increasing amount of government money and attention is being devoted to problems of international concern on which scientific collaboration is feasible, from such combined scientific operations as the International Geophysical Year and the exchange of scientists to the negotiation of agreements concerning the prohibition and inspection of nuclear weapons tests. The range of science covers the complete agenda of government functions, from national defense and law enforcement, and international arrangements for keeping the peace, to maintaining national prosperity, transportation, communication, welfare, and education.

The scientific revolution, then, has had a pervasive effect on the agenda of government. But how has science affected the institutions and processes of American government? In a larger sense, it has had little effect on the basic principles of the American political system: the separation of powers, federalism, judicial review, and the rule of law. Scientists show few signs of wanting to enter elective politics, or of advocating changes in the pluralistic party system of competitive political recruitment. But scientists have vigorously entered the arena of executive, legislative, and administrative policymaking. The President has a special assistant for science and technology on his own personal staff. This person is chairman both of the President's Science Advisory Committee, composed of scientists from universities and nongovernmental research institutions, and of the Federal Council on Science and Technology, an intergovernmental coordinating body composed of the heads or science advisers of the principal federal scientific departments and agencies of the government. The President's science assistant is also director of an Office of Science and Technology, with his own staff; they work with the Bureau of the Budget in developing and coordinating all science programs and financial proposals in the annual budget. Each house of Congress has several committees concerned with science, and they invite distinguished scientists to serve as consultants and witnesses at hearings and conferences on legislation affecting science policy or having important scientific aspects. Advisory councils have been set up by every agency having either a research program of any size or money to grant or contract for research. Thus scientists are represented (1) at the working level of operating bureaus to review research proposals and results, (2) at the higher committee levels to formulate and develop new interagency and extragovernmental programs of scientific research, and (3) at the highest policy levels of government to advise on the scientific aspects of any governmental problem—defense, economics, foreign policy, health, education, and welfare.[9]

[9] National Science Foundation, *Science Organization in the Federal Government* (Washington, D.C.: U.S. Government Printing Office, 1963).

The pattern of American science policy since World War II was formulated in 1945 in an extraordinary report, *Science: The Endless Frontier*,[10] by President Roosevelt's scientific adviser, Vannevar Bush. The basic elements of that policy are:

1. Within the federal government, there should not be any absolute policy of separating pure or basic research from end-use or applied research.
2. Applied research and development should be encouraged by a system of federal contracts and grants with industrial, university, and nonprofit corporate organizations, rather than by the federal government attempting to consolidate and control all research through its own facilities and one central agency.
3. Although basic research cannot be confined to one type of enterprise, there should be an independent government agency, in this case the National Science Foundation, organized and staffed by scientists, which receives and reviews requests for financial assistance from universities and private scholars, to whom it makes outright grants for basic research.
4. Special attention should be given to the recruitment, education, utilization and allocation of scientific manpower.
5. Planning for scientific progress and development should not be centralized at one point, but should seek to preserve diversity and variety in the sources of ideas, financing and expenditure. Coordination rather than centralization of decision-making is required at points as close as

---

[10] Republished by the National Science Foundation in 1960, with an introduction by Alan Waterman (Washington, D.C.: U.S. Government Printing Office).

possible to the President and the key points of Congressional action.

6. Emphasis in science policy should be placed upon allocation of funds for research and scientific manpower to secure the best possible balance of effort in the national interest; and upon a continuing, systematic review of the impact of scientific knowledge on other elements of national policy.

Perhaps the most perplexing aspect of the relation of science and government concerns the question of whether the scientist's view of himself and his calling can be sympathetically felt and understood by the ordinary man. In daily life we rely so heavily upon scientific authority that we are highly upset when we observe the spectacle of scientists publicly disagreeing among themselves, thereby losing the effect of calm, noncontroversial certainty that we expect from high authority. No one really knows how far the general public must understand the habits, attitudes, and motivations of a representative and powerful ruling group in order for this group to maintain prestige, popular support, and the vital cohesion between ruler and ruled that enables the political community to prosper and survive. In democratic societies it would certainly seem that a widespread appreciation of the spirit and methods of scientific inquiry, not merely admiration for its gadgetry, nor fear of its power, is essential to the growth and contribution of science to human welfare. I do not think it necessary, if indeed it were possible, for most people to become scientists to understand the conditions of a civilization based on the values and achievements of science. Trust, belief, and confidence are essential foundations of authority, however, and such relationships should not be founded on false pretensions or misconceptions. The scientists we admire and trust are those who frankly exhibit in their public lives the habits and techniques of inquiring minds engaged in the quest for truth; who do not pretend to omniscience and absolute certainty; who admit that science consists in theories, guesses, speculative hypotheses soaring far beyond the bonds of existing knowledge, as well as self-imposed standards of experimentation and observation to test the validity of these speculations in every way possible. Democratic societies are in urgent need of citizens who comprehend both these aspects of "the scientific mind" at work. If we can accept the curious, contingent, probabilistic conception of science, *not* the mysterious cult, *not* the omnipotent mechanical monster, we may learn to live with science as "an adventure of the human spirit . . . an artistic enterprise, largely motivated by curiosity, largely served by disciplined imagination, and largely based on faith in the reasonableness, order and beauty of the universe of which man is a part."[11] What would a political system be like in which the active citizens view their role as helping government to identify the real problems that impede the realization of their personal and collective development, and as participant-observers they help to formulate the hypothetical solutions (laws and policies) which scientific research proposes to political representatives, administrators, and judges for public test and experimentation?

[11] Warren Weaver, "The Age of Science," in *Goals for Americans,* "Report of the President's Committee on National Goals" (Englewood Cliffs, N.J.: Prentice-Hall, 1960), p. 105; J. Bronowski, *Science and Human Values* (New York: Harper & Brothers, 1956); *idem, The Common Sense of Science* (New York: Random House, 1950).

20 DEVELOPMENT ADMINISTRATION

Merle Fainsod

Development administration represents one of the frontier areas of American political science. A generation ago the term would hardly have been used. Its appearance in the vocabulary of political science registers a new awareness of the administrative problems of the developing nations. Its counterparts are found in the interest of economists in development economics, of sociologists in community development, of students of comparative politics in political development, and of educationalists in educational development. The increasing study devoted to problems of development administration can be viewed as part of a more general concern with the processes of development which pervades but is by no means limited to the American academic community.

The special interest of American political scientists in problems of development administration is largely a by-product of the post-World War II American immersion in global affairs. More particularly, it represents a response of teachers and practitioners of public administration who have been called on by governments, foundations, and international agencies to provide advice and technical assistance in improving the administration of development programs in far-flung corners of the world.

The early experiences of such advisers were not always happy. Consciously or unconsciously, many carried with them their predilections for American ways of doing things, and they tended to assume that remedies developed to meet American problems (and sometimes untried even in the United States) had universal curative powers regardless of local terrain. Gradually the more sophisticated among them began to discover that administrative institutions and practices are reflections of the societies and cultures of which they are a part, and that no program of administrative reform can be viable unless it is adapted to the historical, political, social, and economic realities of the nation for which it is designed. Melioristic experiments thus led the way to greater appreciation of the parochial limits of American experience and wider awareness that variations in administrative behavior grow out of the social, political, and economic contents in which they are enmeshed.

This exposure to the administrative and other problems of the developing nations has affected American political science in various ways. One consequence has been to provide a powerful impetus to field studies of the institutions and political processes of particular nations and areas. Although these studies have by no means been confined to administrative problems, their influence on the study of administration has been liberating in the sense that they have emphasized the degree to which political and administrative problems are intertwined.

The area-studies movement (if one can speak of it as that), which has its outposts in the many area centers that dot the American academic landscape, has enlisted the participation of numerous political scientists who have contributed to and benefited by the interdisciplinary climate in which they work. While the area centers have played a particularly vigorous role in filling out the scholarly map of the developing countries, many useful country studies have also been produced by specialists in government and public administration whose tours of duty in developing nations under government and foundation contracts have given them an opportunity to do their learning on the job.

For political scientists with a particular interest in comparative administration, the developing countries have provided the fascination of a new world of inquiry. The increasing availability of materials on their administrative practices and firsthand exposure to their problems have served to broaden horizons, to plant doubts about the universal application of generalizations derived from Western experience, and to stimulate new efforts at model-building and theory-construction which undertake both to explain the special characteristics of the administrative systems of the developing nations and to relate them to administrative practices elsewhere.

For still other political scientists, whose interests center on the role of administration in economic development, development administration has emerged as a special field of study. Its concern is with the range of problems involved in promoting economic growth and socioeconomic welfare among the peoples of the developing nations. The systematic study of the ways in which administrative instrumentalities can be employed to achieve these purposes provides the subject matter of development administration.

As the term is commonly used, it embraces the array of new functions assumed by developing countries as they embark on the paths of modernization. It is concerned with the machinery for planning, mobilizing, and allocating the resources to expand national income. It has a special interest in the so-called nation-building departments, which undertake to foster industrial development, manage new state economic enterprises, raise agricultural output, develop national resources, improve the transportation and communication network, reform the educational system, and achieve other developmental goals. Defined in the broadest terms, development administration constitutes that part of the subject of public and comparative administration which focuses on the relations between administration and economic development.

Most American political scientists who have singled out development administration for special study would readily concede that they have been influenced in their choice by a desire to see development programs succeed and to contribute to that end, if possible. Many, after experiences in the field, would also add that it is far easier to identify problems than to prescribe remedies. Some have discovered that the goals of economic and political development are not always mutually consistent; that economic growth per se does not necessarily mean a more equitable distribution of welfare; that exclusive emphasis on rapid economic growth may spell political and social disorganization; and that strengthening the powers of development administrators may actually impede and stunt the creative contributions of other groups in society. Almost all have been made aware that what is called development administration has a large political dimension.

Let me define the problem. Development administration is concerned with the economically poor countries. Many have only recently emerged from colonial status; others that have been independent states for much longer periods resemble the new states in that they share a low standard of living, their economies are largely agricultural, illiteracy is high, and the outlook of the mass of the population is traditional and relatively untouched by Western modernizing influences. In varying degrees, they all aspire to higher standards of well-being. The new states face a particularly complex array of challenges. They must build nations out of refractory divisive material; they must establish governments to maintain law and order; they must replace departing expatriates with indigenous personnel frequently untrained to discharge their new responsibilities. Independence is linked with high expectations and new demands for rapid economic progress and a diffusion of welfare benefits and educational opportunities.

The governing elites of the new nations—usually dedicated to modernizing goals—find themselves pressing a series of simultaneous revolutions, overcoming localisms, attempting to transform the traditional fabric of society, developing new symbols of national unity, organizing a political apparatus to guarantee their ongoing power, and launching a development program designed to create a modern economic order. The older underdeveloped states that have undertaken to make the leap into modernity confront many similar problems. They too must undergo a cultural revolution, break the power of traditional elites, and open the way to dynamic modernizing forces.

If changes of this magnitude are to take place without violent disruption, they obviously require political skills of a high order. They also carry with them a heavy state administrative burden. In most of the new states and in many of the older ones, there are no large pools of private native entrepreneurs ready to spearhead the drive for economic modernization. Such administrative talent as exists is largely in state or military service, and such economic resources as are available for development are mostly controlled by governments. The political elites of many of the new nations tend to be collectivist in their orientation; their ambitious development plans involve heavy reliance on the state sector.

As a result, the quality of state administration becomes crucial to success or failure, while impatience for quick results leads to complete disenchantment when they are not forthcoming. In the cautious words of the 1961 report of the Burmese Public Services Enquiry Commission:

> New and ever-increasing demands of a democratic welfare state fell upon a civil service already seriously weakened by the exodus of many experienced officials at all levels. The new rulers . . . were enthusiastic, confident, and infused with a sense of mission. Having led the country to independence, they desired to see their visions of the new Burma rapidly transformed into reality. The new rulers, like the civil servants, were inadequately equipped for the gigantic task of rehabilitation, reconstruction, consolidation and development. In their enthusiasm they overlooked the fact that such colossal schemes as they had in mind took time to materialize. . . .

As the Burmese report makes clear, even when the will to develop is strong among a modernizing elite, development cannot take place until the needed administrative and technical skills become available. Almost every developing nation faces a crying shortage of qualified public servants, teachers, engineers, economists, doctors, agricultural specialists, and trained craftsmen. Even at the level of governmental housekeeping, administration tends to be hampered by a shortage of basic office skills—the absence of filing systems, the lack of trained stenographers, accountants, and office managers, and adherence to antiquated procedures which provide busy work for myriads of clerks but stand in the way of the expeditious disposition of public business.

Still another problem faced by many developing nations is that of maintaining standards of honesty and probity in administering their development programs. Corruption and bribery are by no means a monopoly of poor countries; wherever government salaries are low and the state is the main dispenser of contracts and privileges, there is a special temptation to treat supplicants for government favors as legitimate sources of pay for public servants. Nor is the problem solely one of administrative corruption. The dominant political leadership may use the development program as a source of funds to consolidate its own position, as an opportunity to build up the private fortunes of its leaders, and as a means of rewarding its followers.

At a different level, development administrators encounter frustration when the innovating thrust of their program collides with traditions and customs to which their people are deeply attached. In no area are these inbred resistances to change more firmly rooted than in the villages which still dominate the economies of most developing nations. They are reflected in the difficulties that have been encountered in country after country in modernizing farm practices and in raising agricultural output. They are registered in the disillusionment that has developed around community development programs, because the quick-working miracles which some expected them to perform have not occurred. The realization has been slow to dawn that the modernization of agriculture in a developing country cannot occur overnight.

Here, as the totalitarian countries have discovered, force and compulsion have only limited effectiveness. It is difficult enough to perfect the administrative procedures and techniques which will bring improved seeds, implements, fertilizers, and pesticides to the villages, but it is even more difficult to persuade peasants to use them and to teach them that it is in their own interest to abandon the familiar practices and to embark on what is for them a completely untrod path. In such circumstances, the execution of development programs must depend to a considerable degree on voluntary cooperation. There is no substitute for the slow and arduous process of explanation, demonstration, and persuasion; short cuts to utopia are not at hand.

Still another challenge in development administration is the problem of organizational structure. One of the inevitable accompaniments of development is the rapid multiplication of new governmental functions. As new functions emerge, new administrative units appear which have to be adjusted and coordinated with each other as well as with older departments. The proliferation of new organizations produces such a diffusion of power as to make the task of central direction and coordination extremely difficult.

The problem may be further complicated by a multiplication of public enterprises in the form of government corporations which claim a degree of autonomy not vouchsafed to ordinary government departments. Most developing countries rely heavily on a central planning organization to prepare a coherent development plan, but the degree to which planning is meshed with budgetary authority and machinery for implementation frequently leaves much to be desired. Power rivalries at the center complicate the task of coordination; difficulties traceable to jurisdictional conflicts and lack of qualified personnel at lower levels of the bureaucracy impede the execution of plans.

The political context in which development administration functions will go far to determine its efficacy and success. It is not enough for the political elites of the new nations and the older underdeveloped countries to pay lip service to the goal of development; hard choices and difficult sacrifices may also be required. To build for the future is to rob the present; although foreign aid may ease the burden, it cannot serve as a substitute for a major effort by the developing nation itself. Unless large parts of the nation can be persuaded or mobilized to dedicate their energies to development, development administrators will operate in a vacuum.

How then can the quality of development administration be improved? I referred earlier to the shortage of crucial skills which hampers the progress of many developing nations and gives particular urgency to issues of manpower planning, educational reform, and training programs for the public service. Education and development are intimately intertwined; without a massive investment in education it is unlikely that most developing nations will reach their goals. But education qua education is not enough. The strategy of educational development must gear into the nation's development plans. An educational system that produces large surpluses of graduates in fields for which there is no demand can only end by creating dissatisfied and frustrated groups for whom the very idea of development becomes a discredited farce.

The experiences of a number of developing nations that have indiscriminately expanded their educational systems testify that this danger is real. Clearly the higher educational systems must be organized to provide the array of special skills imposed by modernizing goals. But requirements extend beyond increasing high-level technical competence. At a more lowly, but still fundamental, level there is the need to eradicate illiteracy, to inculcate nation-building values, and to supply an underpinning of elementary job training geared to the development plan. At every stage of education there is the problem of raising standards of academic excellence in the face of overcrowded facilities, overburdened and ill-paid teachers, and inadequately prepared students. Above all, there is the need to jettison old habits of rote learning and to instill an analytic and problem-solving approach adapted to new developmental challenges. Within the broad framework of educational developments, there is a special requirement to improve public-service training and to inject into it a heavy emphasis on subjects related to economic and political development.

It is no easy task to produce the managerial and technical skills required for efficient development administration. It is no less difficult sometimes to create an environment in which such skills can effectively be utilized. Here the political dimension is crucial. It cannot be assumed that all political leaders in the developing nations have a single-minded commitment to pure developmental values. Most wish to remain in power, and, quite understandably, they adapt their development programs to serve this purpose. Most leaders find it necessary to reward their followers, and posts in government and state largesse provide a tempting way to consolidate loyalties. Nation-building may turn out to be a many-sided enterprise in which internal disorders, military adventures, and prestigious expenditures blot out developmental goals.

All this is not to imply that trained development administrators can function efficiently only if they are free of political controls. If their work can be negated when political leaders pursue nondevelopmental objectives, their accomplishments ultimately depend on the political support which they can muster. Without political leadership which identifies its own interests with a high priority on economic development, development administrators are left floating in the air. Development administrators cannot realize their objectives unless they enlist a substantial degree of popular understanding and support. They cannot by themselves manufacture consent. Ultimately they must rely on political leadership and organization to mobilize or release the popular energies which will give life to the content of their plans.

The difficulties encountered by developing countries in the administrative area have led many to search for a quick solution in organizational reforms. Obviously, administrative structures which have grown up in a colonial or traditional setting require large-scale adaptations if they are to be suited to the needs of a developing society. But there is danger in assuming that patterns of organization which have proved their effectiveness in the highly industrialized countries will automatically yield the same results in the developing countries. Every developing country has its own administrative traditions around which a cluster of powerful interests has grown. Sweeping administrative reforms which ignore these interests are doomed to futility; bridges must be built in which the new is integrated with the old. Changes or adaptations in structure require more than the drawing of blueprints. Even though they emerge in response to new problems, pressures, and priorities, they also involve significant redefinitions of the locus of bureaucratic and political power. Reforms cannot be achieved unless the underlying configuration of forces is favorable to such a redefinition.

Progress in development administration is inevitably an arduous task. It is intimately linked with the quality and training of the public servants who are vested with development responsibilities. Progress is dependent upon the existence of a social and political environment which liberates man's energies. Paper administrative reforms can work no developmental miracles where manpower is inadequate and the will to develop is lacking. The secret of development is not concealed in the interstices of administrative structure. It takes place where skill is supported by commitment and the human and material resources exist to translate goals into actualities.

Index

absentee balloting, 140
Adams, John, 28
adjudication, pressure groups and, 151
administration, development, 263–274; force and compulsion in, 269–270
Administrative Procedure Act of 1946, 150
Adrian, Charles R., 196–208
Advisory Committee on Intergovernmental Relations, 178
AFL–CIO, 7
Africa, new political systems in, 16–17; see also emerging nations
age, voting and, 134
Agriculture, Department of, 255, 258
Aiken, George D., 115
Alaskan earthquake, 65
Alexander the Great, 2
American Association of School Administrators, 176
American constitutional system, 20–31; changes in since 1787, 47–48; President and, 43–54; as presidential system, 55; sharing of powers in, 27–29; stability of, 28–29, 47–48, 216
American Farm Bureau Federation, 147
American Federation of Labor–Congress of Industrial Organizations (AFL–CIO), 7
American government, stability of, 28–29, 47–48, 216; see also government
American Medical Association, 7, 145

American Municipal Association, 176
American party system, 118–129; see also political parties; two-party system
American political system, interest groups in, 143–154; see also political systems; politics
American Revolution, 22, 70, 196, 198
antitrust legislation, 34
area-studies movement, 264
Aristotle, 1, 3, 6, 18, 209, 220
Articles of Confederation, 22
Asia, new political systems in, 16–17
associations, 142
Athenians, 3
attorneys, in Congress, 86
Augustine, 4
authority, politics and, 6–8

Babcock, Robert S., 181–195
Bagehot, Walter, 41
Bailey, Stephen K., vii–xiii
balance of power, 27
ballot, kinds of, 140–141
behavior, psychology of, 13
Bentham, Jeremy, 4
Bible, reading of in schools, 39
big business, 127
bilateral agreements, 249–250
Bill of Rights, 23, 36–37
bill(s), committee hearings on, 102–104; committee "mark up" and amendments to, 104–108; filibuster on, 101–105; House floor action on, 110–111; Rules Committee action on, 108–110; Senate and House passage of, 115–117